OPEN
Christianity
Home by Another Road

JIM BURKLO

Rising Star Press
Scotts Valley, California

Rising Star Press
P. O. Box 66378, Scotts Valley, CA 95067-6378
www.RisingStarPress.com

Interior design, composition, and copyediting by Joanne Shwed, Backspace Ink.

Drawings on Part title pages are from a series of meditation cards created by Jim Garrison, and are used with his generous permission. Additional cards may be viewed at the *Open Christianity* Web site, OpenChristianity.com.

Cover design by LeVan Fisher Design.
Original cover art by Barbara Deemy Burklo.

Library of Congress Cataloging-in-Publication Data

Burklo, Jim, 1953-
  Open Christianity : home by another road / Jim Burklo.
    p. cm.
  Includes bibliographical references.
  ISBN 0-933670-05-2
  1. Christianity--Miscellanea. I. Title.

BR124.B87 2000
230--dc21   00-045673

Printed in Canada

for Roberta, who put the poetry back in my life

Contents

Acknowledgements

Writing a book is a solitary activity. Visits with other people are welcome distractions, but the writer must return to focused quietude at the keyboard for long sessions of composing and editing.

But publishing a book is a social—and, one hopes, sociable—process. Many relationships must be developed and nurtured in order to get a book into print, onto bookstore shelves, and into the hands of readers. A book is a product of all of these relationships.

This has certainly been true for *Open Christianity*. I wrote the first draft in solitude; but once the book was on the road to publication, many people had significant roles in shaping it.

Religion is a touchy subject, and my treatment of it was bound to generate some controversy. As I shared drafts of the book with others, they urged me to be more circumspect and gentle in presenting ideas that would offend some readers. My mother, Barbara Deemy Burklo—a journalist and the source of my genetic proclivity to write—said of the final draft that it was "kind." That was as much a ratification of the wisdom of earlier commentators as it was of her motherly pride in my ability as a writer!

The ideas in this book, and the ability to write it, would never have come to me without my 41-year relationship with one good and gifted man, Bruce Urbschat. We have been friends since first grade, and have supported each other in the "examined life" through copious written correspondence.

The members of College Heights Church, particularly those in our Wednesday Watch silent meditation group, also softened and—paradoxically—strengthened my handling of the themes presented here. Jim Garrison provided artistic as well as spiritual inspiration. My congregation generously gifted me with the time needed to write *Open Christianity*, a sign of their commitment to spreading its message. Friends, family members, students at Stanford, and the publisher's review panel also influenced its contents.

This book was refined most of all by Roberta Maran, my wife. From the beginning of this project and through many revisions, she has helped me to keep it honest, to keep the writing congruent with the subject matter.

Being a father has slowed down my writing speed considerably, I'm happy to report. For this I thank my daughter, Liz Burklo, whose zesty, zany personality has distracted me for the past 14 years. I look forward to many more occasions when she will delightfully interrupt my progress at the keyboard.

The publishers, Michole Nicholson and Carl Goldman of Rising Star Press, have become my friends and co-creators in this project. I'm very grateful for their good humor, good business sense, and skill in editing this book into a more readable and interesting form. They have helped me reflect on issues of Christian faith that matter as much to them as they do to me.

Beautiful relationships—those I've named as well as ones too numerous to mention here—have grown in the process of creating this book. I pray that its readers will keep that circle of relationships growing, and that in this small way the book may bring heaven a bit closer to earth.

Jim Burklo
Menlo Park, CA
OpenChristianity.com

Introduction

"I need to talk about some religious questions," he e-mailed me. As a campus minister I have seen similar e-mails from students many times in recent years. But when we met, this young man's story especially touched my heart.

"I don't tell everybody this, but I transferred to Stanford because it's a long way from the college where I started out as a freshman. I needed to get away to keep my sanity," he said.

"I wasn't a particularly religious person—just a nominal Christian, I guess. But my roommate was a fundamentalist Christian, and he invited me to his student fellowship group. I liked the people in the group, liked the focus on matters of the soul. However, it just didn't make sense to me to believe that every word of the Bible was true, or that Jesus physically rose from the dead. They were such sincere and dedicated people, but I could not bring myself to agree with what they said in their Bible studies. Still, I kept hanging out with that crowd, which was a big one on campus.

"After a year or so, I realized I was in a crisis. I had concluded that these students were right. The only way to salvation was through faith in Jesus as shown in the literal truth of the Bible. However, I knew that I could never accept this belief. I would never be able to do what they had done—to step outside my rational mind and take that leap of faith. So I was convinced I was damned to hellfire for eternity.

"My reaction amounted to a nervous breakdown. I became depressed, obsessed with the damnation of my soul that resulted from my unbelief. I had a hard time studying, sleeping, and eating. Why bother with anything if I was going to hell anyway? I knew I had to do something or I would lose my mind.

"So I decided to transfer to another college and get away from those people. I do feel a lot better here at Stanford—this is a much more secular place. Eternal damnation is not in my face all the time like it was before. But now that I've escaped from that pressure, I'm confused. Faith still matters to me, but I don't know what to do about it."

I assured him there was another understanding of Christianity that did not threaten him with damnation, but I could see he was still in a state of shock and disorientation. He wanted nothing to do with organized religion of any kind.

◇

The Christian road leads to such *important* difficulties that people like this young man should not be discouraged from following it because of trivial ones. I have met many people who claim to have no trouble believing that Jesus is the only way to God and that the stories in the Bible are factual. But I don't know any people who find it easy to love God, to love their neighbors as themselves, and especially to love their enemies—a love that sometimes comes at the cost of one's own life.

People succeed in believing the unbelievable much more often than they succeed in loving the unlovable. The Christian way is not defined by declaring belief in a set of doctrines. Nor is it defined by excluding people whose God-given common sense prevents them from affirming these doctrines. Christianity is defined by a road that is hard for everyone who walks it. It is defined by the struggle of Jesus and his followers to love against all odds. A Christian is a person who falls in divine love, fails to love a thousand times, and each time is resurrected by divine grace to love once again.

Unfortunately, in the eyes of that student and of many other people, Christianity has come to be defined as a set of odd beliefs. Most people I know are bored, amused, perplexed, annoyed, or frightened away by these beliefs, and miss the point of Christianity altogether.

My conversation with that student moved me deeply. I wanted to respond more fully to his lament, *"Faith still matters to me, but I don't know what to do about it."* This book is my answer to him and the many others who might follow Jesus' road if they could see their way around an impassable roadblock of unhelpful dogma.

If you are not a Christian, this book invites you to explore the teachings of Jesus without requiring you to accept the Bible as literally true; or to follow an extreme, inflexible, or nonsensical theology. If Christianity is your heritage, this book invites you to love God and neighbor as Jesus did; to abandon or reinterpret any dogma that gets in love's way; and if you have left that heritage, to come back to it with joy.

PART I

Setting Out

Build thee more stately
  mansions, O my soul,
As the swift seasons roll!
Leave thy low-vaulted past!
Let each new temple,
  nobler than the last,
Shut thee from heaven
  with a dome more vast,
  till thou at length art free,
Leaving thine outgrown shell,
  by life's unresting sea.

Oliver Wendell Holmes
last stanza of
"The Chambered Nautilus"
1858

1

Why Another Road?

Christianity is the language of my soul. When I read the gospels, the stories of Jesus in the New Testament, I am captivated by the challenge of living out his love. I've read the Bible regularly most of my life, but every time I open it I find more jewels of insight, more depths of meaning. When I take the bread and the wine, remembering Jesus' Last Supper with his disciples, I enter into a mystical union with God and with everyone throughout history who has ever shared in this sacred feast. The music, the myths, the symbols, and the rituals of the church are food for my heart, giving me rich poetic and artistic forms to express my deepest and best self. My practice of silent meditation is guided by the prayer discipline of Jesus. In the community of the church, I have witnessed the power of the unconditional love that is God. I have seen Christianity elevate the humanity and divinity of people, guiding society in the direction of peace and justice.

But to feel at home in the Christian faith, I have followed a circuitous route: a *new road* to my spiritual home. There were many features of traditional Christianity that I found untrue, chauvinistic, or overly complicated. I was especially disturbed by the claim that Christianity is the one and only true religion. I had to find a way around these obstacles to uncover the valuable components of the faith that call out for our embrace.

◇

According to biblical legend, Jesus was born in a manger because there was no room for his parents to stay at the inn. Today, millions of people are told there is no room for them in the inn of the church because their good common sense makes it impossible for them to accept certain doctrines of traditional Christianity. But just as Jesus was born outside the proper confines of the inn, so can Christian faith today be born outside the confines of traditional orthodoxy. Everyone is invited— shepherds and wise men, conventional believers and doubting seekers alike.

Did the three wise men who journeyed to Bethlehem to pay homage to the newborn Jesus become Christians? We have no record that they ever affiliated with the church or professed the faith. They seem to have gone home and continued their lives as scholars and astrologers. We are told only that they went home to the East by another way, deeply moved by what they had seen. They may not have joined the church or recited its creeds, but they had experienced the Christ. When they met the Christ, "they were overwhelmed with joy." (Matthew 2:10) What response could have been better? It is enough to know that they participated in the beginning of that great movement of the Spirit we call Christianity. My own goal is not to "be a Christian"—an adherent of a particular religion—but rather to "be Christian": to try to love God as Jesus did, while exuberantly rejoicing along with the three wise men.

Many who now seek a way back home to Christianity originally entered it through a traditional form of the religion that they can no longer follow. Others have been discouraged from exploring Christianity at all because their only exposure to it has come from self-promoting evangelists and churches, or the dubious activities of the religious right. A more open form of Christianity is needed to bypass doctrines that are obstacles to a living faith, enabling people to enter into the Christian experience by a nontraditional road.

So to all who feel an affinity with Christianity, yet cannot accept all of its historic doctrines, I offer this encouragement: *you are not alone.* It can be traumatic to leave familiar beliefs and rituals behind. The guilt, shame, and fear associated with questioning the doctrines of a rigidly traditional church can be painful. It can be excruciating to change one's relationship to a community of fellow "true believers," or to grow out of that community altogether. It is tempting to knuckle under and ignore the dissonance between good sense and religious upbringing, or to reject religion altogether. But there are many forms of spirituality and community that can encourage the transition into a much more open form of faith. Together we can reclaim the best that lives within Christianity, and take a new road toward a world culture of spirituality that includes, but transcends, sectarian differences.

This book is a meeting place between Christians who are leaving strict orthodoxy behind, and non-Christians who hope to discover Christianity's rare treasures and enlightening practices. It is also an invitation to a fresh, soulful dialogue. All too often, religious language has the effect of separating people from each other and isolating spirituality into sectarian spheres. Some faithful people use their religious jargon as a way of distinguishing themselves as a separate culture. Others don't mean to isolate themselves from others, but their use of religious language raises a wall just the same. By dropping divisive religious jargon whenever possible, we can return spirituality to its rightful place in everyday conversation.

◈

Tradition and dogma are by no means inherently bad. Taken with a grain of salt and interpreted in historical context, they can be powerful sources of instruction and creative imagery. But when they are used to exclude or deter people from the faith, they become problematic. **In this book, I use the terms "traditional," "dogmatic," and "orthodox" to mean any form of Christianity claiming to be the *only true path* to God**. Versions of this religious orientation can be found within most Christian groups: liberal Protestants, Catholics, evangelicals, fundamentalists, and charismatics. Adherents to this point of view contend that a relatively inflexible Christian faith, as they have defined it, is the only road to salvation for a suffering and sinful humankind.

Asserting that Christianity is the only true and valid religion among the many spiritual paths people have followed throughout history raises hard theological questions. Over the centuries an elaborate, convoluted set of doctrines has been constructed to answer them. *Open Christianity* attempts to blaze a trail past this tangle of doctrines, so the way of the Christ can be made clearer for those who are attracted to that path but have not yet found their way to it.

While I am convinced that it is time to abandon the claim of exclusive truth and to shed much of the complexity of Christianity, I honor what is good along the traditional road of faith. I admire the many Christians who remain loyal to orthodoxy while articulating it in fresh, helpful ways. I honor the soulful compassion and sincere faith of many fundamentalist and evangelical Christians. But to harmonize the truth of the soul with certain traditional doctrines, a great deal of hairsplitting explanation is required. This is why such discourse usually remains the province of clerics, scholars, and a small cadre of intellectually disciplined lay people. They may be successful in their attempts to keep otherwise dead doctrines on life support, but the process is of questionable value.

I cannot believe that a living faith must be so complicated. I cannot believe that God would be so perverse as to necessitate a religion encumbered with bizarre doctrines. Does God really expect us to believe things that require the suspension of our God-given good sense and the expense of so much time studying the arcane details of ancient history? Jesus' own theology boiled down to two essentials: " 'You shall love the Lord your God with all your heart, and with all your soul, and with all your mind.' This is the greatest and first commandment. And a second is like it: 'You shall love your neighbor as yourself.' On these two commandments hang all the Law and the Prophets." (Matthew 22:37-40) Many of my theologically conservative friends are hanging on to doctrines that obscure the light of love that shines from their hearts.

A number of Christian traditions took root in cultures from which we have long been cut off. They are relics of history, interesting as academic pursuits but no longer central to faith. To believe now that the world literally was created in six days, or that Jesus literally walked on water, is an affront to modern scientific understanding, to everyday common sense, and to the ancient culture in which such beliefs had their place. There are many doctrines in orthodox Christianity that served useful functions in their time, but now deserve to be respectfully interred in the reliquaries of the past.

Enduring organizations often depend on a very clear definition of who is "in" and who is "out." A strong sense of community loyalty can develop among a group of people whose beliefs and practices are distinctive. Arcane theological doctrines often have no real value except as ways for churches to maintain clearly separate identities.

For this reason, a Christianity that is liberated from outdated theology will need a new kind of church organization. To exist without traditional orthodoxy, the church needs to break free from its triumphal mission of dominating the planet, putting magnificent sanctuaries in every neighborhood, enlisting lots of members, and raising lots of money. It needs to give up the chain-store approach: a franchise with a strict formula, with a store in every town that delivers the same hamburger everywhere. Instead, the church can become an amorphous movement with no walls; no boundaries; and a flexible, responsive theology. It can take a great number of forms, including the familiar church on the corner, spirit-centered movements for social change, small gatherings for silent prayer in living rooms, worship at rock concerts, readings by authors at bookstores, and shows of artworks that display Christian imagery.

Christianity is a language, not a corporation with a trademarked brand name. Languages have identities, but they are living things that grow and change and shift, always generating new forms of expression. And no "clergy" can control a language; it has a life of its own. People can complain all they want about those who don't speak "proper" English, but we need to remember that the "proper" English of today was the creative street slang of yesterday. Christian language will also continue to change, incorporating fresh insights while abandoning terms that no longer speak for our souls. I hope this book will be a small contribution to that evolutionary process.

◇

In these pages I describe a way of faith that is liberated from some doctrines to which many Christians still cling, to make room along the road for the rest of us. As it has been from the advent of Jesus' ministry, Christianity is changing. More and more people are learning to love God through the story of Jesus, while leaving unhelpful baggage from historic Christianity by the side of the road.

A book that addressed each of the Christian doctrines which bother or bewilder so many people would need to be three times as long as this one—and even that would be no more than an introduction. This book is a beginning, a conversation starter, a first step for those who are looking for a new road to faith.

The book begins with a bit about my own background and spiritual journey. I then consider the traditional ideas and practices of Christianity, seeking enduring as well as new meanings in them, and challenging those that obscure the heart of the faith. This leads to an exploration of Christian spirituality, service, and social action. The book closes with "A Credo for

Christians," which expresses an open form of Christian faith for our time.

Before we proceed, let me offer a warning—perhaps the theological version of an "environmental impact statement." Many people were gracious enough to critique this manuscript before it was published, and provide comments and suggestions. Several of them asked a penetrating question: since I don't agree with some of the most basic doctrines of Christianity, and since I'm proposing a Christology sharply divergent from traditional thought, why do I insist on calling myself a Christian? Couldn't this book just as easily have been titled *Open Any-Religion-At-All*?

My answer is this: through Christ I have learned how to find God. It is through Jesus that I have found the language and the substance that form the foundation of my faith, my spiritual practice, my value system for living. True, the perspective for my worship is not orthodox. But when I look inside, it is Christianity that I find reverberating within my soul. And although I believe there are many paths to God, the path for me is indeed called "Christianity," even if some might argue that it should be given a different name.

Come, let's walk together for a while.

2

My Story:
Discovering Open Christianity

I asked a lot of questions as a kid in Sunday school. While our church was modest in its theological claims compared to many other denominations, it still gave me a strong dose of traditional Protestant Christianity. I complained that the earth could not have been created in six days. I was told that this was symbolic—but symbolic of what? I complained that Jesus' mother could not have been a virgin. I was told this was a miracle, but miracles seemed like cop-outs from common sense. Most of what I heard in church left me confused and disturbed.

In the fifth grade, I decided to get the answers for myself, so I went home and started to read the Bible. It confused me even further. If the Bible were a new book, it would be banned from the shelves of children's libraries. I was terrorized by passages such as this one from 2 Samuel 20: "And Joab took Amasa by the beard with his right hand to kiss him. But Amasa did not notice the sword in Joab's hand; Joab struck him in the belly so that his entrails poured out on the ground, and he died." By the time I was in the sixth grade, I was convinced that while Jesus was a good person, the religion that had built up around him was pretty creepy.

When I was 16 years old, I signed up to go backpacking in the Sierra Nevada range for the first time. I didn't know that the trip was sponsored by a fundamentalist Christian organization. Our leader took us into the mountains, and along the way he led us in Bible studies. Every time he opened his Bible, I argued with him. I challenged every point he tried to make. He responded with a syrupy, patronizing attitude that further provoked my impassioned objections.

All the while, I was deeply moved by the scenery through which we passed along the trail. The beauty of the Sierra overwhelmed me at every turn. This first experience of alpine wilderness was the culmination of my childhood enchantment with the mystery and magic of the natural world. At last we got to the top of Kearsarge Pass, with its spectacular view of the southern range and the jewel-like lakes below. Again, our leader pulled the floppy Bible out of his backpack and started to read.

I thought it was a sacrilege to ruin such a holy moment with religious nonsense, but I sat and listened as he read the heart of the Sermon on the Mount. I felt something I had never felt before. There was a presence within that seemed to have come from beyond me. I felt the love that Jesus talked about when he said, "Love your enemies." I realized it was impossible for me to love my enemies, including people like the leader of our backpacking trip. But while it was impossible, I felt love for my enemies anyway. To live that love was the supreme challenge, worth the risk of life itself. And the natural beauty around me, at which I gazed awe-struck, was suffused with this divine love. There, on top of Kearsarge Pass, I found God . . . or, I should say, God found me.

For the rest of the trip I did not argue with our leader when he began his Bible studies. I didn't say much of anything at all to him. I still disagreed with almost everything he said, but my opinions didn't seem very important anymore. I was in a state of amazement, glowing for days with the warmth of the love that had just been revealed to me. Everything I'd argued about so vigorously before seemed like utter trivia after that moment on Kearsarge Pass, when the love that is God became real to me.

At the end of the trip, I realized that while I didn't agree with him any more than I did at the beginning, the trip leader had been the means through which the love of God had entered my life. I needed to express that love to him. I looked him in the eyes, shook his hand, and thanked him. It was the beginning of my life-long effort to rise to Jesus' challenge of loving my enemies.

◈

Back home, I tried to reconcile my life with my encounter with God on the mountain. In high school I became embroiled in the student activism of the late 1960s. The church of my upbringing didn't have answers to the questions raised by the war in Vietnam—a war that demanded a moral decision from every young man facing the military draft.

One evening, a salesman came to our house to show his furniture catalogs to my parents. He got into a long conversation with me, asking what mattered in my life. When I told him about my involvement in the peace and justice movements, he told me he had been a religious conscientious objector during World War II, performing alternative social service instead of becoming a soldier. He went on to tell me about the Christianity of the Quakers and other antiwar Christians, and about Gandhi's spiritual and political practice of nonviolence. I was electrified to find a connection between the experience of God and the movement for peace and social justice. Among many other books he suggested, I devoured the autobiography of Gandhi, the journal of John Woolman (a colonial American Quaker mystic and social reformer), the life of the Buddha, and the Christian writings of Leo Tolstoy. I discovered that I was not alone. There was a way to interpret the best of the Christian tradition in light of my own experience and commitments.

In 1976, after college, I went to a Presbyterian theological seminary in Marin County, California, intending to explore spirituality. I did not know if I wanted to be a minister. I wanted to gain a deeper understanding of the faith that had helped to form me.

The seminary must have perceived that I was not a very orthodox Christian. I was assigned to share an apartment with a most unusual student. His head was shaved, and he did yoga every morning on the living room floor. He had meditated in a Tibetan Buddhist monastery in Nepal before coming to the seminary.

"What are you doing here?" I asked him.

"After a year and a half in the monastery," he answered, "my lama told me that I had learned everything that he could teach me. 'Go home,' he told me, 'and study in a Christian seminary. You need to learn and practice the religion of your native culture.' "

My roommate contributed enormously to my seminary education. I asked him to teach me how to meditate. Every morning, we awoke at 5:30 and climbed the seminary hill to sit silently in the chapel, with its stunning view of Mount Tamalpais. It was then that I learned the everyday discipline of knowing God. And I experienced the common mystical ground shared among the religious traditions of the world.

After seminary, I was ordained into the ministry of the United Church of Christ. My first job was to serve as the associate minister of the First Congregational Church in Palo Alto, California. At that time, the church expected the associate minister to be an activist for peace and social justice.

During this period, I traveled with a group of Christian peace activists to what was then the Soviet Union. On one of our stops I found myself walking through the halls of the Russian Orthodox seminary in Zagorsk, northeast of Moscow, engaged in a discussion with a Communist Party official. He worked for the Soviet government agency responsible for regulating (and thus discouraging) organized religious activity in his country. He was a charming, highly literate fellow. With genuine curiosity he asked about my religious beliefs. I told him I was more interested in religious experience than in belief. After sharing with him my own inner sense of God, I asked him about his spirituality. He told me mine sounded very similar to his own. He said he had a strong sense of the "otherness" of the universe; a powerful feeling of awe toward the cosmos. We walked together, a committed Christian and a committed atheist, sharing a common experience but using different language to express it.

On the walls around us were scores of hauntingly beautiful icons. These silent testimonies spoke in the ancient language of artistry about the reality that I called God and that he called Wonder. I considered the tragic antagonisms that exist among people around the world who are adherents of various religions and nonreligions, when there is such a commonality of spirit among us all. This moment affected me powerfully, and inspired a lifelong commitment to break down the walls that block people from sharing their spiritual experiences.

Back home, I went on to take jobs at the Ecumenical Hunger Program and the Community Services Agency, which served low-income people. I chaired the organizing committee and became executive director of the ecumenical, interfaith Urban Ministry of Palo Alto. This ministry offered homeless people love, hospitality, and many different forms of emergency assistance. I found myself drinking coffee every weekday morning with the unemployed, mentally ill, and addicted.

Nine years of working with people in crisis resulted in my second spiritual conversion. In the world of homeless people, I began to discover the meanings and metaphors that pervade the gospel stories of the Bible. Jesus became more important to me than ever. I sometimes felt a tingle of anticipation that he might show up in the flesh at our drop-in center, fill a styrofoam cup at the coffee tap, and sit down with us.

Most of the people Jesus encountered were extremely poor, and many of them were also mentally or physically ill. As I worked every day with people in similar circumstances, the Bible began to speak to me in a fresh and forceful way. Among street people, I began to see what Jesus meant when he told his followers to give up their homes and possessions, take up their crosses, and follow him. I began to question many of the assumptions of American culture. The American ideal of getting ahead, of progress, of bigger and better, began to look empty to me; I could see the damage it was doing to the poorest of the poor. I began to realize the truth of the Buddha's saying that all of life is suffering. Around me every day was abundant evidence of the falsehood of the mass-media hype that suggests that everything will be wonderful if you just drink enough of the right soda pop and buy the right automobile. Homeless people opened my heart to the pain of the human condition, and inspired me to practice compassion in my relationships with people just as I practiced it in prayerful meditation.

I now serve as the minister of College Heights Church in San Mateo, California, and as the campus minister for United Campus Christian Ministry at Stanford University. In these roles, I serve people who demand that I reflect upon what works—and what doesn't work—in the Christian heritage. They know there is something in the faith that they need and want. But they struggle with Christian traditions that in so many ways contradict their intuition and common sense. Students and parishioners demand straight talk from me when they ask what relevance Christianity has for living. They want answers in plain English; many of them are allergic to traditional religious rhetoric.

I feel compelled to respond to these needs, because they are my own. Like the students and church members whom I serve, I need to square my life story with the religious story of which I am a part. I cannot reject Christianity without impoverishing my soul, cutting it off from the nourishment that comes through its spiritual roots. But my embrace of the religion is significantly different from that of my ancestors in the faith. I have sought out another Christian road that can lead me to my spiritual home.

Christianity and other religions result from a natural human need to describe the personal encounter with the love that is God. For better or worse, religion often becomes a much more elaborate and complicated thing than the basic spiritual experience that gave rise to it in the first place. It is tempting but deceptive to think that mastering the complexity of religion is the same thing as experiencing God.

Religion should not be taken too seriously. A story attributed to the Buddha tells us that it does not make a lot of sense to carry the raft on our backs down the road after we've used it to cross the river. The raft of Christianity is burdened with obsolete traditions that we now need to drop by the side of the road in order to move freely toward the presence of God. I now invite you to join me in sorting out those traditions that bring us closer to God from those that block our way into the heart of Christian faith.

Clearing a Road Through Christian Traditions

do you have the patience to wait til your mud settles and the water is clear?

Lao-tzu

JG 92

3

Keeping Faith

When I worked at the Ecumenical Hunger Program, an interfaith group that served low-income people, I was responsible for raising money and keeping track of the organization's business affairs. EHP Director Nevida Butler was an icon in the community—a source of seemingly boundless compassion for clients, volunteers, and staff people alike. A former welfare mother herself, she acted as parent, minister, and social worker to thousands of people.

One day, after laboring over the financial records of the organization and concluding that we were headed for a crisis, I went to Nevida's office and explained the situation. She listened attentively to my explanation of why we were in serious financial trouble. Then she looked me right in the eyes and said, in a loud voice that could have thundered from the pulpit in a church, "REVEREND, HAVE FAITH!"

She turned out to be right. I still don't understand how we did it, but we made our budget and met our payroll that year.

Fifteen years after that incident, Nevida still has faith. It is not faith "in" something in particular. It's just pure, raw faith. And it's infectious. After her response, I was speechless. She inspired me to act as if all would work out well, and it did.

What do we really mean when we talk about "Christian faith"? So often we are told that faith is about the assertion of certain doctrines. We are told that it is something you state, as you would the Apostles' Creed. But faith is about something simpler and at the same time much more profound than a mere statement. It is living *as if* all shall be well; *as if* life is meaningful and good.

Too often we live *only if*. We decide that we can be happy only if we have a certain quality of life. We can be happy only if the house is big enough, the mate sexy enough, the car fast enough. The problem with living *only if* is that life never quite meets these conditions. When we live *only if*, we don't really live at all: we spend our time waiting for ever-increasing expectations to be met.

Living *as if* is a bold stance of action and emotion suggesting that the world is a better place than it plainly appears to be. When things look grim, you act as if they aren't so grim. When things look hopeless, you act hopefully anyway. When you don't have what you want yet, you act as if you already have it, and that helps you to get it. Living *as if* isn't a denial of the harsh realities around us. It's a clear-eyed recognition of these challenges, and a self-informed choice to act as if you can or already have overcome them. Living faithfully—living *as if*— gives you the strength and imagination to make the world a better place.

Christian faith is raw faith that is expressed in Christian language. Christian faith isn't about accepting a certain creed. It is, rather, a culture of rituals, stories, and symbols that describe the universal experience of faithfulness. Jesus taught a way to be faithful that worked whether or not a person ever became an official Christian. "Consider the lilies of the field, how they grow; they neither toil nor spin, yet I tell you, even Solomon in all his glory was not clothed like one of these. But if God so clothes the grass of the field which is alive today and tomorrow is thrown into the oven, will he not much more clothe you—you of little faith?" (Matthew 6:30) Christian faith is not about believing that Jesus was God's only Son. It's about living as if we will be clothed and cared for by God as least as beautifully as are the lilies of the field. What makes this faith Christian is the imagery that is used to describe it.

There is a difference between faith "in" Jesus and the faith "of" Jesus. Faith "in" Jesus depends upon our conceptions of him, which are subject to challenge and change. Ironically, too much focus on religious belief can weaken our faith. Students come to my door at Stanford in crises of faith because the campus culture challenges the traditional religious doctrines they once had faith "in."

The faith "of" Jesus is much more durable. The faith of Jesus was raw and tough. His faith had nothing to do with doctrines that could be doubted. Despite the poverty, suffering, and overwhelming oppression that surrounded him, Jesus lived as if his life were eternal, as if his life made a difference, as if he could be useful to the people around him. His faith was a gift from God that gave him the strength to change the world.

4

God:

An Introduction

The first roadblock for many people who encounter Christianity is the vision, concept, and description of God. The vast majority of Americans say they believe in God, but when asked who God really is, the consensus breaks down instantly. Is God one and the same with the universe? Or is God a separate entity controlling the universe? Does God intervene in human affairs? If so, in what form?

The confusion is exacerbated by traditional Christianity's insistence that Jesus, the historical person, was both God and man at the same time. It is easy to get lost immediately in the maze of names and attributes of God: Father, Son, Holy Ghost; Creator, Jesus Christ, Holy Spirit, and so on. I suggest that instead of beginning with an explanation of the myriad Christian doctrines about God, we start by experiencing God directly. Only then can we begin to sort out which Christian ideas about God still make sense.

Twice a week, I sit down for about 45 minutes in a quiet place with my back upright—a comfortable position that will keep me relaxed but alert. I try to pay attention to what is going on in my body and in my mind. What am I feeling? What am I thinking? What urges, images, emotions sweep through me? I watch, I observe, I notice myself. I watch while things happen, fade away, and other things take their place in my body and mind. I try to simply observe, without judgment. I try to accept whatever I'm thinking or feeling, without trying to change anything.

After a while, this observation of myself takes on a loving, caring, accepting quality. If I'm bored, I compassionately observe my boredom. If my mind is jumping from one thought to the next, I have compassion for it. If I'm unhappy about something, I have compassion for my unhappiness. After a while, the compassion takes over and has a life of its own within me. It is as if I am experiencing two selves: the Self that observes, and the self that is observed. The Self that lovingly observes is God. The self that is lovingly observed is my personality, existing in real space and time; and this self is thankful for the compassionate grace that is God.

◈

The essence of religious experience can be encountered without participating in any formal religion. It can be challenging, but it is not complicated. It does not require a lot of knowledge, but it usually requires a lot of practice.

Meditative silent prayer is but one of many forms of this practice. I get a similar experience when I'm able to be truly compassionate, not just superficially polite and friendly, toward other people. In those moments, I experience my true Self as the love that we share. It is as if the "I" that makes up my personal identity is not the one who is doing the loving. It is not my ego that is acting compassionately. As a matter of fact, it is as if my ego falls away, and I *become* the compassion that I share with others. This experience makes sense of St. Paul's words when he said: "It is no longer I who live, but it is Christ who lives within me." (Galatians 2:20)   The Christ is the divine love that human beings selflessly share with each other. I find God again and again in the joyous but challenging discipline of truly loving my wife, my daughter, my family, my friends, and the people around me.

Being part of a community contributes to my personal discipline. On Tuesday and Wednesday mornings, I meditate in the company of groups of people who keep silence together. These circles deepen my commitment to this discipline. We help each other maintain the practice of experiencing God. Together, we amplify our sense of the presence of God in the prayerful silence.

This experience, or something very much like it, has been recounted to me by people from a wide variety of religious— and nonreligious—backgrounds. We may use different language to describe it, but what happens in prayer and meditation is remarkably similar among adherents of all the world's major religions. The experience is available without subscribing to any particular set of beliefs, without joining any formal religious institution, without years of seminary education.

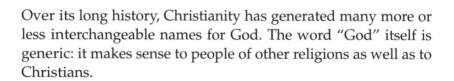

Over its long history, Christianity has generated many more or less interchangeable names for God. The word "God" itself is generic: it makes sense to people of other religions as well as to Christians.

- ◆ In the English Bible, the word "Lord" often refers to God. It is used to translate the words in Hebrew that were themselves used in place of the holy name of Yahweh, the God of Israel. The feudal, patriarchal implications of "Lord" do not fit well with my own experience of God.

- The word "Christ," in Greek, meant "anointed one," referring to the ancient practice of coronating a king by anointing his head with oil. The word "Christ" also referred to the hope of the Jewish people for a Messiah, the long-awaited king who would save his people from oppression. But the word has taken on a new meaning in Christianity. St. Paul makes it clear that everyone is able to let the Christ live within and through them. Since the Christ is the mystical union of God with human beings, Christ has become another name for God.

- The title "Son of God" used to describe Jesus was also a name for God, because in ancient times, firstborn sons identified completely with their fathers. They inherited their fathers' property, occupations, and roles in the community. In an era when firstborn sons are no longer the social or spiritual replicas of their fathers, this name has lost much of its original meaning.

- The "Spirit" or the "Holy Ghost" is also used interchangeably with the word God. The biblical Greek word for "spirit" or "ghost" was *pneuma*, which also can be translated as "wind." The breath of God is God. The Word of God, expressed by this wind or breath, is God.

- Most Christians today believe that Jesus, the historical person of the first century, was in some meaningful way God. This idea gets in the way of experiencing God for ourselves, because it suggests that Jesus was something other than a human being like the rest of us. I believe he found God within himself, and taught others to recognize the divinity at the core of every person's being. But that does not mean that his body and his ego were divine, any more than is the case for the rest of us. We call him Jesus Christ because he had the Christ experience, and led us to the wonder and mystery of his discovery. But that alone does not lead incontrovertibly to the requirement that he was more divine than any other human being.

- The doctrine of the Trinity—Father, Son, and Holy Ghost or Spirit—has perplexed Christians for a long time. It was formulated in the fourth century as a way of settling a long theological and political controversy in the church about the nature of Christ. The doctrine is not to be found in the Bible. It is the result of an ancient philosophical debate that has little to do with spiritual experience, and it is not necessary to believe in it to be a Christian today. But the doctrine of the Trinity does remind us that there are many useful names for God. Each name has a context, each name expresses a different quality of the encounter between God and human beings. As Christians, we have choices about which names for God most eloquently express our encounters with the divine.

- "God is love, and those who abide in love abide in God, and God abides in them." (1 John 4:16)   Love is the name of God that makes the most sense to people who can't relate to traditional religious terminology. Unconditional love, extending beyond the bounds of attraction and affection and family ties, is divine. It is a gift that comes from within us, yet beyond us. A living faith requires nothing more nor less than receiving and sharing this love.

5

God:
Knowing or Believing?

I sat with a circle of students in our evening discussion group at Stanford University. I posed a question to initiate the discussion: "When and how have you had a direct, personal experience of the presence of God?" The answers were fascinating, and each story was different. When it was her turn, a graduate student from Indonesia reported that she had a strong sense of the presence of God every time she read Psalm 63:1-8. So we got her a Bible and asked her to read it aloud.

"Oh God, thou art my God, I seek thee early with a heart that thirsts for thee and a body wasted with longing for thee, like a dry and thirsty land that has no water . . ."

The group fell into a rapturous silence as the very tone of her voice conveyed the meaning of the psalm. I could not help feeling the love of God soaking into me like rain into the desert sand. When she finished reading, she said with a radiant smile, "It is so romantic, this psalm. You could substitute your boyfriend's or girlfriend's name for the name of God, and it would be a love song. Every time I read it I am overwhelmed with the loving presence of God."

The most basic idea in Christianity (or almost any religion)—that God exists—is a stumbling block for many people who find no proof for this assertion. But there is a Christian road that transcends this problem.

Belief in God can be an unsatisfying intellectual exercise; *knowing* God is a heartfelt spiritual exercise:

- When I find hope alive in seemingly hopeless situations, I know God.

- When I witness love that transcends friendship, family bonds, or physical attraction; when I witness love for enemies or love for the unlovely, I know God.

- When I witness sincere effort for the cause of real justice and peace, I know God.

- When I am in the midst of a community of people who put their egos aside, honor each other's souls, and seek divine truth through loving action, I know God.

- When in meditation and prayer, I cease to identify myself with my own personality, and begin to feel compassion toward all people and things, I know God.

I do not need any proof for the existence of God. I do not need to believe that God is the Master Designer or Chief Executive Officer of the Universe, manipulating everything on earth, directly or indirectly. Instead, I know God as a compassionate presence. I long for that divine presence like a dry and thirsty land longs for water. This presence is more than an "it," which is why I describe God as a person whose being transcends the human categories of gender. My heart is touched and warmed by God. My knowledge of God is not a conclusion I reached as a result of weighing the evidence for and against the existence of a deity.

◇

"How do you know God? What happens to you when you meditate or pray or otherwise explore your inner life? How does it feel? What effect does it have on you and on your relationships with others?" Such questions evoke answers that reveal a great deal of shared experience among people. By contrast, asking "Do you believe in God?" courts argument.

My experience of God cannot be proven, nor need it be. I can't prove that I am happy, but when I'm happy, I'm sure of it. And when other people tell me they are happy, I'm inclined to take their word for it. So it is with God. I have no proof for God's existence, but I am certain that I have encountered God. Efforts to logically demonstrate the existence of God just get in the way.

But while it is not a matter that can be rationally tested, my relationship with God is not irrational. It does not conflict with my intellectual faculties; it does not contradict good common sense; it does not fly in the face of logic or science. On the contrary, my experience of God leaves me with a keen sense of the mystery and wonder of the universe, which makes me intensely interested in scientific exploration.

God is not a necessary hypothesis for any question that most scientists would deem worthy of study. This does not contradict spiritual experience; it merely delineates the sphere of science from the sphere of religion. But there are some scientists who go too far, denying the spiritual dimension altogether and reducing our conscious existence to a pattern of synapses firing in the brain, no more significant than neural activity during a drug-induced hallucination. We know better in our hearts: our encounters with God convince us that the universe is a meaningful place.

But just as scientific inquiry won't answer important questions about meaning, value, and purpose, we are on shaky ground when we invoke God to explain how the universe works. Religion cannot replace science. We trivialize God when we attribute certain phenomena to divine action, relying on beliefs about God to fill in what science cannot yet explain. The universal religious sentiment of awe before God suggests that while we can know God, we cannot know everything that God knows. Our profound sense of the otherness, the mystery, of God implies that a complete knowledge of God's purposes will always remain beyond us.

In order to honor the sacredness of our encounter with God, it is best for us to keep our beliefs *about* God to a minimum. God alone is holy—not our ideas about who God is, or what God wants us to do. God alone is worthy of worship. We stray from the road of faith when we worship religion itself, as if it were the divinity to which it points. The map is not the territory.

The mere existence of the question "Do you believe in God?" indicates the extent of the breakdown of traditional Christianity. Only a few centuries ago, such a question would have sounded absurd. Virtually everyone in the Western world believed in God. God was the most necessary of all hypotheses. The fact that anyone asks the question today suggests that we are developing a new understanding of God for our time. The rapid evolution of science, the exercise of our powers of reason, have made us unsure of the nature of God as Creator. But the inner working of the divine spark in the human soul remains much the same. The spiritual experience of human beings has changed very little over the millennia.

When I read the writings of the ancient mystics of Christian tradition, it seems to me that their words could have been written yesterday. So when I speak of God, I do not ground what I say in a system of beliefs about the details of God's personality, nor about the precise manner in which God acts as Creator. Instead, I ground it in the verity of my own experience of God and in the divine encounters of other people throughout history.

Trying to find the basis for faith in scientific or philosophical proof of God's existence is a lot like Yuri Gagarin's declaration after he returned from the first manned voyage beyond the atmosphere. He found evidence for the official atheism of the Soviet Union: "I'm sorry to say that I didn't see anyone. In fact, I don't think there was anyone to see to begin with." If you define God in a narrow way, you are likely to miss the divine presence.

Instead of seeking proof or disproof of God's existence, I suggest another approach: pursuing the intimate knowledge of God that Jesus experienced and offered to all of us. If we are secure in our heartfelt knowledge of God, we will have no need for pseudoscientific arguments for and against the reality of the divine.

◇

St. Paul went to Athens to preach the gospel. There, among the statues of the various gods of the Greek pantheon, he found an intriguing altar. It was dedicated "To an Unknown God." Paul declared to the Athenian philosophers that the Unknown God could now be known. He said this God could not be depicted in images of metal or stone, "formed by the art and imagination of mortals." (Acts 17:29)   But traditional Christianity risks becoming—in some instances, has become—the same kind of religion Paul decried when it worships the Bible and the Christian religion itself, both "formed by the art and imagination of mortals," as if *they* were God. It is time for Christianity to return to Athens and worship once more at the altar of the Unknown God, who cannot be fully described in human terms or forms, but can be found and known in every human heart.

6

Jesus:
Unique and Universal

It was springtime at Red Rock State Park in the Mojave Desert of California. I was on one of the desert pilgrimages I take at least once a year. After a predawn cup of coffee cooked on the campfire, I hiked up to the top of a hill of crumbling pink rhyolite, looking east as the sun rose. Below was a ribbon of shallow, silvery water meandering through the bed of the wash at the bottom of the canyon. Purple and yellow wildflowers defined the edges of the stream. Overwhelmed with the scent of the moist sand, I stood reconciling and "re-membering" myself to God for another day.

I strayed off the trail toward a cliff to look at the rocks, and then walked up a dry wash. In the brush, I suddenly noticed a strange flower growing all alone. It was a mass of tiny purple blooms on a mushroom-shaped trunk, no more than 6 inches tall. I got down on my hands and knees and stared at it awhile, amazed. Then I got up and walked for a long time, not seeing a soul, before returning to my camp.

In the evening I met my neighboring campers, two deeply tanned "desert rats." We talked about our shared love of the desert.

I described the flower I'd seen, asking if they knew its name. "Oh, we saw that flower, too," they said, "Pholisma arenarium." They showed it to me in their wildflower guide. Then they identified the same location where I had found it. The three of us were shocked. In that huge landscape, far off the trail, one flower had drawn us to itself against all odds. One flower commanded our worshipful attention, embodying all the beauty that beckoned us into the desert in the first place.

A particular flower in a specific place, admired by three unique witnesses on a special day. For us, there was nothing generic about that flower, though it was certainly not the only exemplar of its species. Nor is any individual person generic or mass-produced, despite the fact that there are nearly six billion humans on the planet. It may be hard to remember in the face of the relentless media barrage to the contrary, but each human being is unique and therefore incalculably valuable.

Many people have a hard time with Christianity because they object to its claim to be the one and only true religion, with Jesus Christ as the one and only source of salvation. If this were the only interpretation of the faith, I'd reject it, too.

But Christianity says something else, something deeper. It speaks to what a parent feels for a child. This baby is everything; the universe turns at the point of the birth of this little individual. Likewise, the Christian gospel turns on the story of a particular individual named Jesus. Christianity says that if you're looking for God in the abstract realm, you're going to find yourself in a hall of mirrors. People who say they don't believe in God are often saying that God can't be found through the reasoning processes of science and mathematics, and they are right. God is personally, subjectively experienced by human beings through particular people and events.

Each religion has a special insight to offer humanity, and Christianity's is this: God showed up among us through a unique individual in an idiosyncratic manner in the midst of history. Jesus, born in a backwater of the Roman Empire in an otherwise undistinguished time, discovered that his true inner Self was the Son of God. To his followers, he was so important that it seemed he was the one-and-only Son of God. But he isn't the only one-and-only Son of God. This seems paradoxical, but it makes sense every time I look at my daughter. To me, she is the one-and-only best kid on earth. But I know she isn't the only one-and-only best kid on earth, any more than I am the only adoring father on the planet. When I meet another father who thinks his daughter is the best one on earth, he and I understand each other completely.

The story of Jesus describes the universal human condition in an extraordinarily profound way. If there is such a thing as a miracle, the myth of Jesus is one of them. I am much more impressed with it than I would be if I saw somebody walk on water or if I saw somebody rise from the dead. Modern technology can enable us to do such things, but it can't manufacture a gospel.

◇

I love Jesus, that spiritually awakened, compassionate, irritable, intense, witty, brave, rash, articulate young man who still shakes up the world. Reading about him in the biblical gospels, remembering him in the rituals of the church, meditating on him, imagining him: he lives in my soul. The stories and teachings of Jesus move me like no others. I often feel a presence—as if he were standing just behind my shoulder—as I read the gospels. My relationship with Jesus has shaped every aspect of my life. Jesus has influenced my career choices, the way I relate to other people, and the way I understand the meaning and purpose of life. When I stumble, the story of Jesus is there to help me pick up the pieces and learn from my mistakes. Wherever I go, whatever I do, the influence of Jesus pervades every aspect of my life.

But my relationship with Jesus has evolved. The Jesus I know today is so much more real to me than the one I knew in Sunday school. I have had to critically examine the traditions about his life in order for him to find a place in my heart. I have had to discover the myth of Jesus that rings most true with my soul and the souls of people around me.

In our culture, we tend to discount the value of myths. Loving a mythical Jesus might seem inferior to loving a factual Jesus. On the contrary, I have found that myths are very often more important than historical facts. They are stories that crystallize human experience, and make sense out of the disparate and seemingly disconnected details of our lives. They make life whole: they give it meaning and reveal its purposes. The gospel—the story of the life of Jesus—is an exceptionally potent myth.

We might have a much easier time reading the gospel story of Jesus if it were as blatantly mythological as the fanciful stories about the ancient Greek pantheon. But in the case of the gospel of Jesus, we are dealing with a myth that is based partly on history, and it is extremely difficult for even the best Bible scholars to separate all the myths from all the facts in the New Testament. The gospels were a genre of literature that freely blended the two.

Because practically nothing else was written about him in the first century besides what is found in the New Testament, the Jesus of history is hard to know. The solid evidence about him is sketchy. If we limit our experience of Jesus to those facts about him that are historically verifiable, that are not biased by the axes that his early followers had to grind, we won't be able to have much of an experience of him at all. In order to know and love Jesus we must use creative imagination to come up with myths about him, even if those myths may be at odds with the descriptions of Jesus that are touted as certainties by traditional Christianity.

Ever since his death on the cross, and maybe even during his life, people have been inventing and reinventing Jesus.

Although he was most certainly an historical person, the Jesus we know and love today is mostly mythological. And whether or not we care to admit it, we do have a choice about which of the many myths of Jesus we will let into our hearts. When we talk about Jesus with other people, we need to examine which Jesus we are considering. This isn't always an easy thing to do, especially with those who are convinced that their Jesus is an historical certainty.

The traditional Christian Jesus might be compared to a fictional superhero—an all-powerful, all-knowing, sinless God in human disguise who acted as if he were mortal when he really was not. Support can be found in the Bible for this kind of Jesus. But there is a tantalizing alternative. The Bible also offers a Jesus who is much different from the traditional understanding of his title, "Lord and Savior."

The first hint of this alternative understanding of Jesus is found in the story of his baptism in the Jordan River by his kinsman, John. At that moment, the "Holy Spirit descended upon him." (Luke 3:22) The experience immediately drove him into the desert to meditate and fast for 40 days. He sensed great power in himself there, and was tempted to exercise it wantonly. He had a vision of all the kingdoms of the world, and felt tempted to claim authority over them, but he rejected the pursuit of that kind of power. He was tempted with paranormal powers of the body and mind, but he rejected pursuit of those powers as well. Jesus' final response to these temptations was: "Do not put the Lord your God to the test." (Luke 4:12) In other words, during his 40 days and nights in the desert, Jesus discovered that his true Self was God, and there could be no point in tempting God. At this point, according to the gospel (Matthew 4:11), "suddenly angels came and waited on him."

In the desert, Jesus had the same experience that countless people have shared before and since: the awakening of the innermost soul to its divine nature. He found God within himself. This is called a "mystical" experience, not because it is mysterious or supernaturally magical, but because, as the dictionary says of the word, it relates to "an individual's direct communion with God or ultimate reality." In the desert, Jesus became one of the greatest mystics of history. Once he knew who he was, once he was sure about his true Self, he returned from the desert and began his itinerations as a rabbi and healer.

Sometimes obliquely, sometimes directly, as he traveled and taught, Jesus told his listeners that he was God. Many people thought this was blasphemous. They misunderstood him, thinking that he meant that the personality called Jesus was the same as his innermost Self. This misunderstanding continues to the present day. He answered them: "Is it not written in your law, 'I said, you are gods'? (Psalm 82:6)   If those to whom the word of God came were called 'gods'—and the scripture cannot be annulled—can you say that the one whom the Father has sanctified and sent into the world is blaspheming because I said, 'I am God's Son'?" (John 10:34-36)   Jesus suggested repeatedly that his experience of his innermost Self as God was something available to those who came after him: "The glory that you have given me I have given them, so that they may be one, as we are one, I in them and you in me, that they may become completely one . . ." (John 17:22-23)

Jewish tradition taught that a person could not see the face of God and live; that is why Moses had to veil his face when he encountered God on Sinai (Exodus 3:6). But Jesus was a fully human being who saw the face of God within his own soul, and lived. And he taught that all of us can do the same, and truly live.

Jesus asked his disciples, "Who do you say that I am?" (Mark 8:29, Matthew 16:15, Luke 9:20)   Another time, he said "Very truly, I tell you, before Abraham was, I am." (John 8:58)   He was awakening his followers to the difference between his limited, mortal personality and his unlimited, immortal, divine nature. It is no accident that when Moses asked the identity of the presence in the burning bush on Mount Sinai (Exodus 3:14), the answer was "I AM." The ancient Hebrew name for God, Yahweh, is a form of the verb "to be." God is Being, the essence of existence, the true Self within every burning bush, every burning human soul. "I AM" is the Lord; "I AM" is the Savior. Jesus knew that his true Self was "I AM," and he taught us to recognize that the same is true for the rest of us as well.

Jesus had discovered that his true Self was the Christ, but that didn't make Jesus a perfect human being. The gospel—the good news of Jesus—is that a normal, flawed human being can discover God within him or herself. Jesus' imperfections are *necessary* for the gospel myth to have any power for me. In the gospel stories of the New Testament, I find a Jesus who had bad days. Sometimes he was arrogant and short-tempered. Like every good teacher and spiritual guide, he had a vision that was bigger than he was. Unfortunately, much of the religion that formed around him turned him into an unrealistic idealization. Although traditional Christianity claims that Jesus was both perfectly human and perfectly divine, to suggest that he was perfect at all is to deny his humanity.

The tradition tells us to emulate Jesus, to live as he lived. But if he was perfect, then he was not really one of us. This presents us with a hopeless situation. We are supposed to be perfect, as he was, but we are told that Jesus was the unique Son of God, the one-and-only perfect human. So even though traditional Christianity declares that through faith in Jesus we are forgiven of our insufficiencies, our state of insufficiency is categorical and permanent because we can never be the sort of being that Jesus was. The result of this belief system is unnatural guilt and shame, a tendency to wallow in our inadequacies as we repeatedly ask forgiveness for them. This extra load of shame and guilt breeds low self-esteem, which breeds more sin, which breeds more reasons for feeling shame and guilt. Belief in a perfect Jesus can be harmful to the health of our bodies, minds, and souls.

We need to stop groveling before God. It is true that evil dwells in us all, but we need to stop defining ourselves as hopeless sinners, because it prevents us from taking up our God-given responsibility for our own actions. Self-respect means owning up to our failings and humbly invoking the presence of God within ourselves for help in doing life differently.

And we need to remythologize Jesus in a way that restores him to his true humanity. In the gospels, we can see there were times he behaved dubiously, just like the rest of us. One time he was hungry, saw a fig tree that wasn't in season, and withered it with a curse (Mark 11:12-14). There was the time he was told that his family had come to visit him, and he brushed them off, saying that his family consisted of those who did the will of God—perhaps not the nicest way to treat one's mother and brothers (Mark 3:31-35). On another occasion, he compared a Gentile woman to a dog licking up crumbs below a table (Mark 7:24-30). These stories are important elements in the myth of Jesus that ring true for me, because they remind me that he was just as human as anyone else. His body was subject to the same biochemical rushes of rage and lust as other human bodies. His ego was subject to the same inflation and deflation as the egos of the rest of us. His failings make him realistic, enabling me to feel a strong and palpable love for him. Recognizing his faults makes his love for me even more vivid, as well.

All too often, Christians are focused on Jesus as a master of special effects: walking on water, raising people from the dead, magically healing people of illnesses. But this version of Lord and Savior is exactly the identity that he rejected during his 40-day retreat in the desert. Repeatedly during his ministry, people expected him to be an all-powerful king. Repeatedly, he disabused them of this notion when it surfaced.

In John 14:6, Jesus said, "I am the way, the truth, and the life. No man comes to the Father except through me." Traditional Christians usually interpret this quote to mean that you must have a very specific Christian belief in order to get right with God. This is one of the foundations of the chauvinism that has caused so many people to see the church as rigid, excluding, and dismissive. Traditional Christianity holds that we can't get to God directly, the way Jesus did. Rather, we must go through Jesus and the Christian religion to get to God.

I don't believe the traditional interpretation above is what Jesus meant at all. I find a much different meaning in the words, "No man comes to the Father except through me." Who was the "me" through which people come to the Father? Jesus of Nazareth, the mortal personality? Or the Christ, which was God within him and everyone else? I read Jesus to mean that no one comes to God except through encountering God within him or herself, the Christ experience that is "the way, the truth, and the life."

You are not going to find God "out there." You can't prove God's existence with objective evidence. You can't offer a logical argument that will enable you to reason your way to God. You can't present a theological doctrine that will deliver God on a platter if you just accept it. You don't get to God automatically by saying "Yes" when you are asked if you accept Jesus as your personal Lord and Savior. My student friend whose story is told at the beginning of this book had a deep intuition that saying "Yes" to this simplistic question would have been profoundly dishonest. A person can get accepted into the traditional Christian club, but won't necessarily find God that way. Jesus taught us to get to God through a direct mystical encounter. When Jesus returned from his meditations in the desert, he no longer thought of himself as being only Jesus of Nazareth, the mortal personality. From then on, he identified his true Self as the Christ who lived in him. Christ was his inner experience of God as the ultimate ground of his being.

Jesus constantly asked people to do impossible things. He asked them to love their enemies (Luke 6:7). He asked them to take up the cross and follow him (Mark 8:34). He told them to give up all their possessions (Matthew 19:23-26): "Jesus said '. . . it is easier for a camel to go through the eye of a needle than for someone who is rich to enter the kingdom of God.' When the disciples heard this, they were greatly astounded and said, 'Then who can be saved?' But Jesus looked at them and said, 'For mortals it is impossible, but for God all things are possible.' " Jesus taught that we need to recognize God within ourselves, identify our deepest Self with God, and stop clinging to our mortal personalities with all their attachments. The rich man, as a rich man, cannot enter the kingdom. Only the deeper Self within the rich man, the divine nature within him, can enter the kingdom and be united with God. And Jesus wisely observed that the rich—those who are wealthier, sexier, stronger, and smarter than others—are also more likely to cling to their egos. Jesus was asking the rich man to give up something much more difficult to abandon than his wealth. He was asking him to release his attachment to his own mortal personality.

As a personality, I cannot love my enemies. If I did, they would not be my enemies anymore. My ego is partly defined by my conflicts with these people. The only way to love my enemies is for me to give up my ego, and identify with the Christ who lives in me. As a personality, I cannot take up the cross and follow Jesus. It would be self-destructive to do so. To meet Jesus' challenge, I need to give up my ego self and take on the Christ Self. As a personality, I cannot give up all my possessions. To meet Jesus' challenge, I need to find a way to stop letting my possessions define who I am, and let God define me.

Jesus asked the people around him to join him in this ongoing process of ego abandonment and self-discovery. Over and over again, he gave up the identity of king or Superman, wonder-working hero and political savior. Over and over again, he chose the path that St. Paul described: "It is no longer I who live, but it is Christ who lives in me." To say that the historical personality named Jesus is the Almighty Master of the Universe is to miss the point of his teaching and example.

Traditional Christianity reads the Bible and sees one Jesus, while I look at the same Bible and find another. For better or worse, historical research and textual criticism are not going to resolve the difference. The Jesus Seminar is a group of Bible scholars who are trying to clarify who the historical Jesus really was, and what he really said and did. Their scholarship has ignited controversy because it shows how few of the words attributed to Jesus in the Bible can be verified as accurate. While this kind of scholarship is valuable, I believe that the myths about Jesus have always mattered more to people than the scant reliable evidence about the historical Jesus. Discovering Jesus begins when we see that we have a choice about how to know and love him. Our hearts can tell which myths ring most true. And the Jesus who rings true for me offers an open invitation to a beautiful and meaningful life, not to a place of eternal torment, for my student friend and all others who yearn for a new expression of faith.

7

Spirit:
Watching Whirlwinds

My widowed grandmother lived in an old house in Taft, California, that my grandfather had purchased and towed into town from the oil fields. It had been the cookhouse on an oil lease in its previous life. The bats and boards on the outside of the house were so desiccated that it seemed the place was held together mostly by the paint that covered it. Everything in the house was covered with a fine layer of dust. My grandmother was a fastidious housekeeper, but the dust was omnipresent nonetheless.

"Those dust devils!" she would complain. "There is no way to keep this place clean." It was the thing she hated most about the desert. I thought the desert was wonderful, and the dust devils—whirlwinds that scoured the scrubby hills around Taft—fascinated me every time I visited Grandma's place. But I didn't live year-round in a house that could never be cleaned, haunted as it was by spirits of sand, ghosts of grit.

The dust devils would churn up the desert and sweep it into town. They had no respect whatever for the city limits and the chain-link fences around the yards of the residents of the town of

Taft. They unerringly infiltrated doorjamb gaps, knotholes in siding, windowsill cracks, keyholes. When my dad was young, people paid him to paint their cars in his shop, which his father had salvaged from the oil fields. But sometimes dust devils spun toward the garage, through the corrugated edges of the galvanized iron walls, and ruined his work. They covered the freshly painted cars with sand and gave them a texture that made them microcosms of the surrounding landscape.

The dust devils of the California desert are the same as the djinns or "genies" of the ancient Near East. The djinns were whirlwinds, like the one out of which God replied to Job's complaints, and like the one that lifted Elijah off into heaven. The idea that whirlwinds in the desert are physical manifestations of spiritual beings is an ancient one.

If you're trying to paint a car or clean a house, a djinn is a maleficent spirit, indeed. Apparently the oil field roughnecks of Taft did not think to make three requests each from the genies that passed them by. They only noticed that whirlwinds blew dust into their Spam sandwiches. So they called them "dust devils," obnoxious spirits that could blast grit through the hinge-cracks in a lunch pail.

There is nothing bad or good about the wind, in and of itself. The same strong wind can blow down one house and spin a windmill to generate electricity for another. Once it gets moving, the wind seems to focus more and more of its energy. It sucks up dust and spreads dust with equal ease.

◇

Spiritual discipline generates energy by focusing the life-force. Prayerful meditation concentrates physical and mental energy, gets it moving in one direction rather than dissipating it through too many urges and ambitions. But this spiritual gift of clarified and one-pointed power can work for both good and evil ends. Just because a certain spiritual practice is Christian does not mean the power that results from it cannot be used destructively.

The Judeo-Christian myth of Lucifer, or Satan, is based on this ancient insight into the nature of spiritual power. According to the legend, when God ordered the angels to bow down to the human beings he had created in his own image, Satan refused. Satan believed that the angels were superior to humans, and that humans should bow down to them. Lucifer was cast out of heaven for his disobedience and fell to earth. Out of his rage against human beings, who he believed had usurped his rightful place as a godlike being, Satan has been using his God-given spiritual power to work revenge against us ever since.

Lucifer, or Satan, represents our refusal to look for the divine image in the human beings around us. Whenever we act as if *we* are made in God's image but certain other people are not, then we are playing the role of Satan. When we take the divine power that is freely available to us, and use it to put down other people in word or deed, we are acting "satanically." Too often the worst crimes against humanity are committed by people who were once considered angelic, gifted with great spiritual power.

The line between positive and negative use of spiritual energy is a fine one. Because we live in a culture that in so many ways denies the existence of the soul, we can be easily mesmerized by people who manifest spiritual power. Our thirst for spiritual communion is so extreme that it sometimes overwhelms our ability to discern whether the power of the soul is being directed toward good or ill. When spiritual leaders use their gifts to abuse others with such acts as sexual impropriety or embezzlement, it often takes much too long for their followers to confront them. No one wants to believe them capable of such evil.

Belonging to a faith community can help us discern good from bad uses of spiritual power. A friend of mine has struggled his entire adult life with schizophrenia. He first exhibited symptoms of mental illness in the 1950s when he was a student in a prestigious university. He began having visions of Jesus so real, so palpable, that sleeping, eating, and studying didn't matter to him anymore. The response of those around him was to call in the men with the white jackets, who took him to the state mental hospital nearby. There he was (as he puts it) "tortured" dozens of times with electroshock treatments. Those were the days before patients' rights were given much respect, and before other effective treatments were known for mental illnesses. For all its horrors, the shock treatments did alleviate some of his symptoms. He was able to get and hold a clerical job until he retired.

He continues to have a very strong and palpable sense of the reality of Jesus. Sometimes he has visions and hears voices. But over the years, he has learned ways to integrate his intense religious experiences with behaving in a socially appropriate manner and taking care of his own practical needs.

"My church has saved my life. Whenever I find myself getting very excited or very upset about anything, I find two or three of my fellow church members and check it out with them. Am I getting carried away with this or that emotion? They tell me honestly what they think, what they see. They keep me sane." He takes Jesus at his word that "where two or three are gathered in my name, I am there among them." (Matthew 18:20) He trusts the manifestation of the Christ in those two or three people even more than he trusts the intense visions of Jesus that appear in his imagination.

The ability to discern positive from negative uses of spiritual power is itself a spiritual gift. "And we speak of these things in words not taught by human wisdom but taught by the Spirit, interpreting spiritual things to those who are spiritual." (1 Corinthians 2:13) I have been astounded by the ability of individuals suffering from crisis or trauma to interpret spiritual energy. It seems that when people suffer terrible loss or shock, they are often forced to become conscious of their own spiritual dimension. They discover, often painfully, that they are spiritual beings. This enables them to notice the finer nuances of the spiritual dimension in other people.

Encounters with very troubled people have repeatedly challenged me to look at my own spiritual energy. Such people often have an uncanny ability to read between the lines of what I say, and interpret the deeper meanings of what I do. They can tell if I am emotionally honest with them. They can tell when I am really in a worse mood than the one I am trying to project. They can see through my small talk. They can read my heart like an open book, even when I want it to be a closed one.

Trauma and crisis can result in this gift of reading or interpreting spirits. But with practice, we can invite this gift for ourselves without having to suffer homelessness or disease, tragedy or addiction. Everybody is spiritual, but a comfortable life makes it easy to forget our deeper nature, easy to ignore the subtle but profound movements of the spirit.

PART III

Clearing a Road Through Christian Scriptures

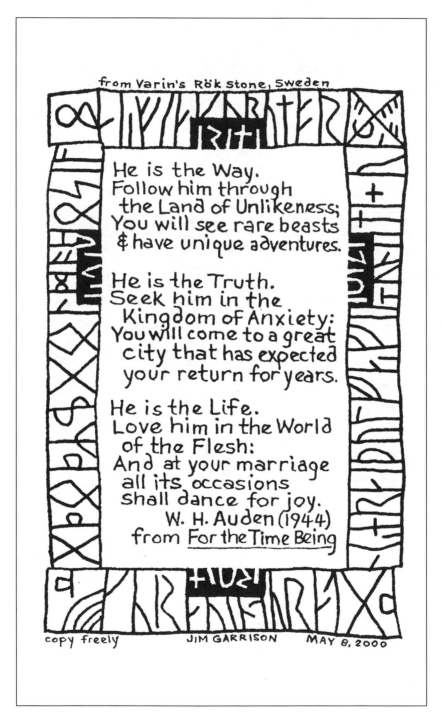

from Varin's Rök stone, Sweden

He is the Way.
Follow him through
the Land of Unlikeness;
You will see rare beasts
& have unique adventures.

He is the Truth.
Seek him in the
Kingdom of Anxiety:
You will come to a great
city that has expected
your return for years.

He is the Life.
Love him in the World
of the Flesh:
And at your marriage
all its occasions
shall dance for joy.
W. H. Auden (1944)
from For the Time Being

copy freely   JIM GARRISON   MAY 8, 2000

8

The Gospel Truth

They didn't really know each other, except as familiar faces from
the streets. She was a young woman, homeless, struggling with an
alcohol addiction but managing to keep herself mostly neat and
clean and usually employed, if only through a temporary agency.
He was a Vietnam veteran whose alcoholism led him literally into
the gutter. He lived in the creek bed not far from the Urban
Ministry's drop-in center. Every day he would gather enough empty
cans out of trash bins to trade in for money to buy a case of cans
full of beer. He wore filthy clothes, had some gaps between his
teeth, and had one finger that was deformed by jungle rot.

On this morning, he came to the drop-in center to sober up
with a cup of free coffee. She came to get a bus pass and a referral
for a shower at the local gym, grab a bite of breakfast, and use our
phone to call her temp agency. Suddenly his eyes rolled back and he
fell to the ground in a seizure. His body stiffened and his teeth
clamped down on his tongue. She immediately rushed to his side,
got a cloth to push between his teeth, and as he heaved and
twisted, she calmly tended him. She put his head in her lap, patted
his hand, and stroked his head until the seizure passed.

That woman's act of kindness was one of the most beautiful things I have ever seen. It's the gospel truth.

The gospel is true not because Christianity is the one true religion. The gospel is true because you can find it in the stories of people's lives, anywhere, anytime. It is the story of one alcoholic loving another through their shared suffering. The gospel is the universal story of the relationship of God and people. Christianity rings true because it tells one version of the many forms that the gospel truth takes in the world.

The original Greek New Testament word for "gospel" is *evangelion*, which literally means "good news." It is not an unbiased piece of professional journalism or a scientific explanation of things. Rather, it is a mythic and poetic story that makes a bold assertion *as if* human life is essentially purposeful, meaningful, and good. Bad things may happen in life, but life itself is blessed. The gospel takes a stand. It is good news because it is a faithful declaration of the positive value of human life.

The gospel accounts of the New Testament declare that the love that is God appears through human life and prevails over the forces of death. The story itself is older than Christianity, and appears everywhere today, if we have the eyes to see it and the ears to hear it. The gospel is not just about Jesus. It is about everyone and anyone who discovers divine love in human life and follows it.

Consummate works of literary art, the New Testament gospels are holographic in their structure. If you break off a piece of one of the gospels, reading a story within the story, you will find the whole gospel contained in that piece. Each of the parables of Jesus is a microcosm, a fractal dimension, of the whole gospel: "To what should I compare the kingdom of God? It is like yeast that a woman took and mixed in with three measures of flour until all of it was leavened." (Luke 13:20-21)   Leaven was ritually unclean for the Jews, and women were considered inferior. Yet through the life-affirming action of the woman and the yeast, the world was being transformed into the realm of the divine.

The biblical gospels are impregnated with yeast. Each pinch is a small story in the larger story, leavening the whole story. And the gospel story, as it is read in the Bible and is found and shared in everyday life, leavens the world today and extends the boundaries of the realm of the divine.

As the gospel is contained whole in each of Jesus' parables, so the gospel itself is a parable. It is a pithy story that gets inside the mind and heart and does things there that the reader does not expect. Reduced to the form of a parable, the biblical gospel might look like this:

To what shall we compare the realm of the divine? It is like a man who was born a commoner, but people thought he was a king. He told them he wasn't who they thought he was, but they kept hoping he would take the throne and be their ruler. Instead, he wandered the world doing good things for people, loving and laughing and crying. Along the road, he found God in himself and the people around him. Because he would not be the person the people wanted him to be, the people he helped turned on him and had him killed. But when he died, they grieved at what they had done. In their grief they found God in themselves and in the people around them, just as he had. So they carried on where he left off, doing good things for people against all odds, loving and laughing and crying.

There are infinite numbers of ways to tell this parable, to share this gospel. A story doesn't have to make any reference to the biblical gospel at all to still impart the gospel message. Here is another parabolic approach:

To what can we compare the realm of the divine? It is like
fruit that grew in a grove of trees on two acres of land. In the
middle of the land was an elegant house in which lived a
corporate executive and his wife. The executive worked 60
hours a week and traveled all over the world on business. His
wife spent lots of time in France buying antique furniture and
in Istanbul buying Oriental rugs. The executive and his wife,
since they had no time for such things, hired a gardening
service to maintain their property. They told the head gardener
that he could do anything he wanted with the fruit from the
trees, since they had no time to pick or eat it themselves. The
head gardener hired a team of undocumented workers from
Mexico to do all the physical work. Every day, they manicured
the plantings and trimmed the trees, and in summer and fall
they picked the fruit and ate it for lunch. The work was hard,
but the laborers enjoyed the serenity and beauty of the
property. At the end of the day, they took home boxes full of
extra fruit for their families, who were crowded into little
apartments in the barrio on the other side of the freeway.
There they enjoyed the fruit with their wives and children.

The kingdom of heaven is not a piece of property that a person
can buy and own. The gospel tells us it belongs to those who
perceive it, work for it, and taste its fruits, no matter who they
are or where they are from.

The gospel needs to be liberated from its protective custody
in the Bible. Just because the gospel is at the heart of Christianity, it does not mean it belongs only to Christianity. The gospel
has a life of its own. It appears in the most usual and unusual
places, subverting our conventional ways of thinking and feeling. It turns our world upside down and empties us so that we
will have room in our souls for the kingdom of heaven.

To be "evangelized" really is to be "gospelized"—to open eyes to see and ears to hear the gospel in the everyday world. Once you are "gospelized," you are able to look past all of the grim evidence to the contrary and perceive the possibilities for love. Seeing the gospel all around us enables us to live *as if* life is good, giving us the hope and strength we need to create the realm of the divine on earth.

9

The Fig Tree:
Another Reading of the Bible

In the Community Kitchen dining room, while passing the serving line on his way for seconds, Dirty Bill took me aside. "Jim, I've been reading the Bible lately and I found the passage where Jesus curses the fig tree. You know, it seems a bit out of character for him to do a violent thing like that. You've been to seminary, you're a minister; explain this story to me."

Dirty Bill did a lot of reading, but this was the first time I heard that he read the Bible. Bill lived in a Pinto with his dog, his banjo, his telescope, and the rest of his worldly goods. When he was an electronic engineer, he had paid a friend to mill him that banjo out of solid brass. But once he hit the streets, Bill spent his days playing the banjo in the park, reading books, and watching the trees grow. Whenever I stopped to talk with him at the Community Kitchen, we would share our observations about the amazing ways of nature. He'd pull out the telescope and people would stand in line in the parking lot to look at the moon through it in the twilight. Bill displayed a vivid awareness of the habits of birds, the qualities of plants, and the changes of seasons as reflected in the heavens and experienced by him while living in his car. Subject as he was to the weather and other elements of nature, he noticed much that I would have missed.

Dirty Bill was so named to differentiate him from other Bills who ate at the soup kitchen where I worked in the early days of my career. I first met Dirty Bill when another homeless man brought him by the agency office to set him up with a meal pass. Most people came into my office for the first time because they needed and wanted something: food, jobs, showers, soap, or just a cup of coffee and a listening ear. But Bill was different. He asked for nothing. He didn't hustle for his survival. He was absolutely courteous and well spoken, and in no hurry for anything. He seemed not to be driven by passions or bad habits. He didn't grasp for life, and depended totally on whatever means of survival landed in his lap.

One evening after dinner, I asked Bill how he was getting along. "I have no idea how I get along. It just happens!" He waved his big arms, gesturing the downpouring of daily grace from above. "If the food or the gas runs out, it just comes! I wake up in the morning and to my amazement, I am still alive. I have no idea how I make it."

According to the calculations of the rest of the Kitchen patrons, Bill had not taken a shower for six months. The blackened dead skin on his arms showed in patches under his arm hair. Three hundred pounds of Dirty Bill stuffed into an old Pinto sedan every night with a poodle and a few opened cans of tuna from the agency food closet; the force field around him was so powerful that few could penetrate closer than two chairs away without choking. Three months before, I had given him a pass to our free clothes closet, and handed him a towel, soap, and a shampoo bottle. He never showered, but he got a clean shirt and wore it, and we celebrated. Three months later, the new yellow polo shirt was blackened down the chest, and his same old Levis were stiffer with dirt.

"What do you think? Why did he dry up the fig tree?" asked Bill.

The story had always intrigued me as well, but I had not reflected upon it with anyone before that conversation with Dirty Bill. I pondered the passage: "And seeing in the distance a fig tree in leaf, he went to it to see if he could find anything on it. When he came to it, he found nothing but leaves, for it was not the season for figs. And he said to it, 'May no one ever eat fruit from you again.' " (Mark 11:13-14)

My mind quickly went into action with Bill's, and I speculated on an aspect of the story that I'd never considered before. "I don't understand the story, either. But it might be about timing. The Greek word for 'season' is *kairos*, which also means the right or appropriate time for something to happen. Jesus was on his way to Jerusalem for the last time when this incident happened. The story might have been an illustration to his disciples that now was the right time, the *kairos*, for bearing fruit, because now was the hour of his passion and death. He was telling them that now was the time for Israel to bear fruit, or never."

Bill nodded, pleased with this interpretation. "I figured it had to be something literary. What's that word in Greek, *kairos?*" I wrote it out for him on the back of a scrap of paper; he could pronounce the Greek letters, because he had once studied a little Greek himself. I was pleased to have been asked the question and to have given such a clever answer.

On my way home in my own Pinto sedan, which was the same year and color as Bill's, I continued to meditate on the story of the fig tree. As I did, I had to admit I still did not understand the story. It was still disturbing, still a side of the personality of Jesus that I didn't like. Why did he wither up the tree, depriving some hapless householder of its fruit in its own right time?

And then the more important question surfaced. Why was Dirty Bill so interested in this story? I had not bothered to find out why he read the story of the fig tree, and why it bothered him enough to ask me about it. Was Dirty Bill himself the damned fig tree—a fruitless, smudged lump of a man who had no season, no hope of coming to bear? In my pleasure at my interpretive ability, I had missed the point of reading the Bible at all: to reveal and describe what is going on around us now. I had missed the opportunity to reflect with Dirty Bill on our life situations and on what the fig tree story had to do with us. I had succumbed to the temptation to be in the helper-client, teacher-student relationship. I had succumbed to the temptation to settle with answers instead of living with questions.

The story got no less disturbing as I spent more time with it. At home I read the different versions of it, and other related passages.

In this biblical story, everybody blew it. First, the fig tree missed the extraordinary opportunity to offer the hungry Jesus some fruit. Think how wonderful it would have been to be able to serve a meal to the Christ! But the fig tree was busy growing out its leaves, and refused to speed up the process for Jesus' sake.

Then, the troubling actions of Jesus himself. He was having a bad day. He was homeless and hungry and about to find himself in big trouble in Jerusalem. He was in such a foul mood that he cursed the tree—which any local person would know was not ready to bear fruit—so thoroughly that it died overnight.

Jesus' disciples were no better. Did they offer food or comfort to Jesus, who was clearly in a stressed, emotional state? No. They asked, "How did the fig tree wither at once?" (Matthew 21:20) The disciples wanted to know how the trick was done, because all they cared about was power. They wanted to do deeds as awesome as the ones Jesus did. They didn't care about the immediate situation and Jesus' need.

And I blew it, too, completely missing the opportunity to listen to Dirty Bill's story as revealed in the account of the fig tree. All I cared about was solving an intellectual problem and showing off my answer, demonstrating my ministerial professionalism, and thinking I could serve another person without becoming deeply involved myself.

I had missed Bill's *kairos*, his right time, for sharing his life.

Once Bill was a Silicon Valley engineer, making good money. Once he had a piano, and played classical music with interesting and educated friends. Now he lived on the streets and played banjo for Bruno, his dog, up at Cuesta Park. He survived off fortuitous encounters with helpful street people, picking up the stray day-labor job or dollar for a gallon of gas or a hamburger. Did he blame Jesus for his withering? Did he blame God for drying up his life, killing his will to live and bear fruit?

I wanted to know who or what cursed Bill and caused him to wither? Was it true that he would never bear fruit again? Would Jesus ever lift the curse from the fig tree? I waited for the rest of the story, trusting it would come in its own right time.

Bill's withering continued as long as I knew him. We did eventually have some "right times" for deeper kinds of sharing, for which I was grateful. I learned more about the reason for his withering: he suffered from clinical depression. I lost touch with him, but I never lost touch with the lesson he taught me that day about the deeper purpose of reading Scripture.

◈

The Bible is a wellspring of stories and images that bubble up afresh with every reading. Reflecting upon it together gives us a mirror in which we discover the meanings of our lives. The Scripture story helped me ask questions about Dirty Bill's story, and examine my relationship with him. Used in this way, the Bible is a living thing that can enrich our souls.

I am able to take the Bible seriously because I don't take it literally. And I am able to cherish it because I do not read it as the *only* authoritative Word of God. But dogmatic Christianity reads the Bible through the lens of its doctrines, and this has the effect of fossilizing the Scripture. It claims that the Bible, as seen through this lens, is the truth, the whole truth, and nothing but the truth—the definitive Word of God for all time. But there are always new "right times" for the Bible to speak to us with new meaning.

Fundamentalist and evangelical Christians claim that their beliefs are derived from their reading of the Bible, but the reverse is just as true. What all of us see in the Bible is in large measure the consequence of the belief system that we bring to it. Traditional Christians claim to find evidence for the truth of their doctrines in Scripture, *but only those people who already share those doctrines can be convinced that the Scripture proves them.* They think the Old Testament points incontrovertibly to its fulfillment in the New Testament, but this is an unconvincing circular argument for many thoughtful readers. Those who say that the Bible is factual, either in every detail or in its most important points, offer as proof the Bible itself, as interpreted by them.

Traditional Christianity is largely blind to the fact that it reads its faith into the Bible. I have a respectful understanding of those who cannot face this fact; if they did, the whole edifice of dogmatic Christianity would disintegrate—a frightful prospect for a large group of people. Questioning or losing their faith would leave them spiritually adrift and might separate them from their churches, where social identity is often centered. They might be alienated from their families. Without belief in the absolute authority of the Bible, they have good reason to believe they would become lost souls.

I recall a long theological conversation I had with a group of undergraduates at Stanford. One of them, considering the consequences of my understanding of the Bible, asked: "How can we count on anything, if we can't count on the factual truth of the gospels? If the Bible isn't true, Christianity must be a lie!"

Challenging the historical accuracy of the Bible is very threatening to traditional Christians, because it calls so much into question. It is hard for them to imagine the possibility of

Christianity having any meaning at all if the Bible is not literally true. I assured the student that Christianity is alive and well on the other side of the question of the authority and nature of the Bible. You really can be a sincere, devout, faithful Christian without having to take the Bible literally when it says that the universe was created in six days, or that Jesus was born from a virgin, or that he physically rose from the dead.

But I could tell that it was going to take a lot more than my words to convince the student that it was safe to question the factual truth of the Bible. After all, people don't become traditional Christians because they read about it in the Bible. They accept traditional orthodoxy because they come into contact with traditional Christians, who are mostly wonderful people who welcome new folks into their church communities. People become Christians because they find a spiritual and social home in the church. In some denominations, the church interprets the Bible for them, and they accept whatever biblical doctrines are given to them because they are presented as an essential part of the Christian package.

In other words, it is through traditional faith and church life that people come to a traditional interpretation of Scripture. Likewise, it is through contact with communities of Christians taking another way that people are likely to begin reading the Bible in a freer manner while keeping their Christian identity. To get over her blindness to the deeper nature of Scripture, this student will need to take the risky step of venturing out in search of an alternative form of Christian community. It is not a simple matter of judging intellectual arguments about the Bible on their own merits.

As part of my own walk away from traditional Christianity, I have had to respect the sociological difficulties related to the narrowness sometimes found in rigidly orthodox church communities. Arguments are useless. Rather, the love of the Christ evidenced through the lives of Christians who are working hard to create a new form of the faith will attract traditional Christians to something beyond orthodoxy.

In our society there is no escaping the Bible, even if we aren't aware of its effects upon us. Its influence on our language and institutions is all-pervasive. Unfortunately, the Bible is not an easy book to understand. There are some passages in it that are immediately intelligible to the modern reader. But the earliest meanings of many biblical stories are shrouded in history. In order to appreciate it in any depth, the reader needs to study sources beyond the Bible itself and learn quite a lot about the culture, language, philosophy, and even the science of the ancient world.

For instance, even if you take the Bible literally, you might think of Jesus' phrases "You are the light of the world" (Matthew 5:14) or "The eye is the lamp of the body" (Matthew 6:22) as poetic images or metaphors referring to spiritual truths. However, in these passages Jesus' meaning was probably much more literal than even the most ardently fundamentalist Christians might presume. It was "common knowledge," a "scientific fact" in Jesus' time, that subtle light emanated from the eyes, interacted with the visible world, and reflected back into the eye, resulting in the experience of sight. People in that time believed that human beings literally had a kind of fire inside their eyes, and that seeing was a very active process. This was the common belief until Leonardo Da Vinci, after careful observation, concluded that the human eye was dark inside. With such historical background, some of the original meanings of scriptural texts become accessible.

Familiarity with biblical scholarship helps to bring the Bible alive, and gives us a sense of how the world looked to the people who wrote its books and letters. When I studied Greek, the original language of the New Testament, I saw that the Bible was a human document. It was obvious that it was written by real people with axes to grind, with biases and opinions, with imaginations, with passions and commitments, living in a culture that was strikingly different from our own. I realized then that the only way to be a truly biblical Christian would be for me to adopt the culture and mind of first-century people living around the Mediterranean Sea. I would need to believe that light emanated from eyeballs, that the earth is a slightly convex plane at the center of the universe, and that above it are stacked seven movable crystalline domes with gem-like planets attached to them. Since I cannot accept these and many other ancient assumptions, I can't possibly be a Christian in the first-century meaning of the word. My identity as a Christian must be based on something other than the literal text of the Bible.

But traditional Protestant Christianity is founded on the idea of the authority of the Bible. So it becomes problematic to suggest that the Bible cannot be taken literally due to its defunct assumptions, or that it cannot be fully understood without reference to a culture that no longer exists. Liberal Protestants waffle on the subject, claiming that the Bible is the basis of their Christian identity, while recognizing that the Bible is full of myths and metaphors based on obsolete understandings of the world. Evangelical and fundamentalist Christians, with varying degrees of conviction, declare that the Bible was, is, and ever shall be the literally true Word of God, and that any confusion we encounter is the result of our ignorance of the mind and purposes of God. But this kind of Christianity is based on relatively recent interpretations of the Bible that are very much at odds with what serious scholars now know about the cultural milieu of the biblical era. What theologically conservative Protestants call biblical truth is not rooted in the early church's understanding of Scripture in the first century, but rather on interpretations colored by Western culture from the sixteenth through the early twentieth centuries, when the doctrines of fundamentalist and evangelical Christianity were fixed.

It helps to look back into church history to make sense of the present dilemma of Christians regarding the Bible. The first Christians did not have a canon, or official list, of Scriptures. Instead, they had a wide variety of writings that circulated among the early congregations. Some of the texts they used have been lost or forgotten. A fifth-century church council generally established the scriptural canon, but the question of which writings were to be included in it was not finally settled until the sixteenth century. This became the Bible as we know it today. Many of the writings that had been circulating in the church up to that time were rejected on political grounds; the churches that most valued them were in disfavor with the Roman church hierarchy. The Bible was created primarily to exclude and reject writings associated with groups that did not conform to the orthodoxy of the Roman church.

At that time, the authority behind the Christian church came first from the hierarchy of the church itself. The church's authority was based on apostolic succession. Jesus ordained his disciple Peter to be the founder of the church, and Peter ordained successors, and so on through the centuries. The authority of the Bible was secondary: it was the church's creation, to be officially interpreted by its bishops and priests.

This changed during the Protestant Reformation which, not coincidentally, happened at the same time the printing press was invented. The early Protestants waged their struggle against the corrupt Roman church hierarchy, arguing that the authority of the church rested in the Bible, not in the popes, bishops, or priests of the church itself. For the first time, lay people were able to buy printed copies of the Bible. For the first time, the Roman church hierarchy had real competition—from the Bible itself. Because of the huge variety of interpretations they gave to the Scripture, the Protestants splintered, and continue to splinter, into a bewildering array of sects.

For centuries, in European and American households, the Bible was the first and often the only book to rest on the mantel. It was the basis not only of religious faith, but also of literacy and culture among common people. It became the basis of modern ideas about democracy and the rule of law. As the law of the church derived from the Bible and not from the word of the Pope and his bishops, so the secular law replaced the authority of princes. While Catholics today continue to focus their worship on the Eucharist—the bread and the wine of Jesus' last Passover supper with his disciples, consecrated and administered by the clergy—most Protestants center their worship on the reading and interpretation of the Bible.

In the past few centuries, however, the church has experienced another crisis. Modern scholarship and research have revealed a huge gap between traditional interpretations of the Bible and the original meanings and historical contexts of biblical writings. At the same time, the rise of science and technology has marginalized the role of the Bible in Western civilization. The Bible appears to directly contradict many of the assumptions of modern science (and the modern culture deriving from that science), and it is clear that our society takes science at least as seriously as it takes traditional religion. Our legal and political institutions have developed far beyond their biblical roots as well.

In the eighteenth and nineteenth centuries, this evolving crisis became fully evident. In reaction, traditional Christians froze their interpretations of Scripture and turned them into rigid dogmas. Evangelical and fundamentalist Christians of today are nostalgic for a Bible-centered era that has forever passed.

Many of these Protestants, reacting to the loss of the Bible's authority in the world, are practicing a religion that might be called "bibliolatry"—the worship of the Bible. This practice confuses the Bible with the Holy Mystery to which it refers. A critical, scholarly reading of the books and letters of the Bible will quickly reveal that most of its writers never intended their words to be part of a larger Bible at all, much less to be objects of reverence.

The Word of God, as described in the New Testament, is something quite different from the Bible itself. The Word in biblical Greek is *Logos*, the expressive and creative manifestation of God. In the first chapter of the gospel of John, the *Logos* is described as the force behind the creation of the universe. Nowhere in Scripture is the Word of God equated with the Bible. Indeed, there is no suggestion within the Bible that there ever was or ever would be the book that we now call the Bible.

The Jews and early Christians who wrote the New Testament books and letters believed that the Law—the first five books of the Old Testament—was the holy inspiration and expression of God. However, the assumption that the whole Bible is the Word of God, and therefore a manifestation of God himself, is not to be found within the Bible. The Christian Bible was the early church's extension of the Jewish concept of Scripture, expanded to include the books that the church deemed most important, and to exclude the ones that were either less valuable to it or most threatening to its organizational integrity.

Still, traditional Christianity presumes that whether or not the writers of the books of the Bible knew it, their hands were being guided by God's. Likewise, they presume that the church councils that picked which books would be part of the Bible were also guided directly by God. Some dogmatic Christians believe that every word of the Bible turned out exactly as God intended; others believe that, while the authors and editors were divinely inspired, they made some mistakes in rendering details. It is as if the biblical writers were legal secretaries who occasionally erred while taking dictation. Of course, this point of view poses the question of why we should presume that the writers of the books of the Bible were any more inspired by God than any others. Was the hand of the writer of the Gospel of Thomas—a very important first-century Christian text which didn't make it into the canon of Scripture—guided by God or not? By what criteria do we tell whether or not a writing is divinely inspired?

As a writer myself, I am quite interested in this question. There are moments when I feel that I'm not the one doing the writing, but rather my fingers are being used to express something on the keyboard on behalf of Someone Else. I'm the canyon through which the river flows; I'm neither the water nor the source of the water. And when I read the writings of other people, whether in the Bible or in modern poetry or prose, I often sense that the words come from a source deeper than the egos of the authors. The writers are openings through which divine inspiration wells up and overflows. I am sure that this phenomenon is real, although I have not found a foolproof way to judge whether or not a particular writing is divinely inspired.

In the Bible, I find a great deal that fails to satisfy my thirst for divine inspiration (for example, the legal hair-splitting of the book of Leviticus). But I also find a great deal that seems to come directly from the heart of God. The ecstatic writings of the Old Testament prophets, the gospels with their unique and almost crystalline structure, the mystical epiphanies of Paul—I have no doubt that these writings come from a much deeper place than the conscious thoughts of their writers.

The Bible as a whole is truly one of the great wonders of the world, a treasure of immense value. Surely its existence can be attributed at least in part to divine inspiration. But Christianity does not depend on the assumption that the river stopped flowing when the canon of Scripture was sealed by the early church. Contemporary writers can be inspired by God just as much as were the writers of the Scriptures. Intuition, the gift of discernment that comes from God, enables individuals and communities of faith to know whether or not a particular writing has the authority of divine inspiration.

While the New Testament doesn't have much to say about the question of the divine authority of the Bible as a whole, it reveals a great deal about the way early Christians looked at the Holy Scriptures they inherited from the Jews. In order to make sense of the life of Jesus in terms of the traditions of Jewish Scriptures, early Christians used a Jewish method of interpretation called *midrash*. *Midrash* assumed that every Old Testament story had layers of meaning, and that new ones might yet appear. The top layer was the literal meaning of the text, viewed as factual history. However, this was seldom considered the most important meaning of the text. *Midrash* presumed that in addition to the scriptural text itself, there were traditional stories that embellished it or explained it. For example, the Old Testament does not give us more than a few hints about the story of the fall of Lucifer, or Satan, from the heavenly court of angels. The traditional image of Satan, assumed to be integral to the gospel truth of modern dogmatic Christians, is based mostly on non-scriptural *midrash*. Beyond offering these extra-biblical stories, *midrash* went deeper, finding multiple levels of allegory or metaphor in each Old Testament passage.

An example of this method can be found in a medieval Jewish interpretation of a passage from the book of Genesis. On the sixth day of creation, after forming the animals and humankind, "God saw everything that he had made, and indeed, it was very good. And there was evening and there was morning, the sixth day." (Genesis 1:31)   The Hebrew word for "the" was the fifth letter of the Hebrew alphabet and also expressed the number "five." Rashi, an eleventh-century French rabbi, interpreted this to mean that the entire creation was conditional upon Israel's acceptance of the five books of the Torah (the first five books of the Old Testament). If Israel had not accepted the Torah, the whole creation would have reverted to primordial chaos. This earth-shaking conclusion is miraculously unpacked from one unremarkable Hebrew word: "the"!

Jesus himself applied *midrash* to the Old Testament. He asked the chief priests and elders in the temple in Jerusalem: "Have you never read in the Scriptures: 'The stone that the builders rejected has become the cornerstone; this was the Lord's doing, and it is amazing in our eyes.'? Therefore I tell you, the kingdom of God will be taken away from you and given to a people that produces the fruits of the kingdom. The one who falls on this stone will be broken to pieces; and it will crush anyone on whom it falls." (Matthew 21:42-44) Jesus lifted two passages from the Jewish Scriptures (Psalm 118:22-23 and Isaiah 8:14-15), completely out of historical and literary context, and conflated into one the Psalmist's rejected corner-stone and Isaiah's stumbling stone. Jesus embellished these biblical images of the stone by adding, "it will crush anyone on whom it falls"—a line that is not to be found in the Old Testament texts. Jesus clearly implied that he was that cornerstone, stumbling stone, and crushing stone. Jesus relied on the time-honored tradition of *midrash* to use biblical images freely and poetically to express his ideas.

After Jesus' death, the writers of the New Testament used this same technique of interpretation to express the significance of his life. The writer of the letter to the Hebrews does *midrash* on Genesis in order to describe Jesus as a high priest. Hebrews Chapter 7 freely and fancifully interprets the story of Melchizedek in Genesis 14:17-20. Melchizedek was the chief of a tribe in the Middle East who sided with the emerging Jewish tribe under Abraham in battles with other peoples. At one point, Melchizedek, in his role both as chieftain and priest of his people, blessed Abraham in a ceremony with bread and wine. Abraham in turn offered Melchizedek a tenth of his wealth. This, and a one-line reference to him in the Psalms, is all the Old Testament has to say about Melchizedek.

But the pre-Christian rabbis did not stop there. They noticed that no genealogy was given for him in the Scripture, nor was there any mention of his death. Therefore, the rabbis suggested, Melchizedek was an eternal being. It would be as if a person were declared to have eternal life because nobody could find his or her death certificate! The Letter to the Hebrews takes it further: "Without father, without mother, without genealogy, having neither beginning of days nor end of life, but resembling the Son of God, he remains a priest for ever." (Hebrews 7:3) The writer of Hebrews claims that Jesus was a high priest for humanity—a priest of the order of Melchizedek—making a perfect sacrifice of himself to expiate the sin of humanity. *Midrash* started with a conclusion and worked backward, unabashedly ignoring the contexts of the stories that provided its supporting arguments.

Few modern Christians use *midrash* to interpret Scripture. Unlike the ancients who did not make such hard-and-fast distinctions, we separate fiction from nonfiction, truth from myth. Today, we tend to assume that each passage in the Bible has one unambiguous meaning, and we want to know what it is. We differ only in how we find it.

Fundamentalist Christians look at the Bible as a timeless, transparent book of literally true stories and eternally binding precepts. Want to know what to do about abortion, or capital punishment, or homosexuality? Just look it up in the concordance, find the chapter and verse, and there is the answer, plain to see. Liberal Christians tend to look at the Bible with an eye to separating fact from myth, studying the cultural milieu of the biblical era, and using historical and scientific methods to reconstruct the most "reliable" or "original" versions of the texts. Bible scholars try to separate what Jesus really said or did from the amendments of later editors or copiers of the New Testament. What the ancients saw as rich inspirations for allegory and artistry, modern Christians sometimes see either as immutable truths or quaint but inspirational relics.

A frequently seen bumper sticker says, "God said it, I believe it, that settles it." But this is not the approach that was used to interpret Scripture in biblical times. Scripture didn't "settle it" for people in Jesus' day. The ancients didn't assume that there was only one thing that each passage of Scripture really meant. Instead, the people in Bible times thought of Scripture as a holy, immutable raw material given to them by God so they could make fresh leaps of imagination in their interpretations. Scripture was a fixed language for expressing new experiences in ways that might stray far from whatever original meanings the text might have had. For the ancients, the Scripture was a lot like our *Webster's Dictionary*. It was a source book, a set of images and stories that could be used to express nearly anything one needed to say.

When Jesus was 12 years old, he ditched his parents after a pilgrimage and stayed behind in Jerusalem. "And after three days they found him in the temple, sitting among the teachers, listening to them and asking them questions. And all who heard him were amazed at his understanding and his answers." (Luke 2:46-47)   This passage suggests that he asked questions and got answers from the rabbis, and that they asked him questions which he answered. It was a creative dialogue, not a rigid catechism. It was an art form at which Jesus excelled. In the Temple, Jesus had been participating in the endless *midrashic* discourse about the meanings of the Torah, and there he might have remained, except for his parents' intervention.

We can bring back the lost art of *midrash* by doing to the New Testament what the New Testament writers did to the Old Testament. My viewpoint is not at all the same as that of the writers of the New Testament, but that doesn't mean I shouldn't creatively employ their images and stories to express my own experiences. After all, that is exactly what the early Christians did with the Old Testament—with flair, they used it to express ideas that never entered the minds of the people who wrote the Jewish Scriptures.

And, through *midrash*, we can transcend questions of fact versus myth. There need be no contradiction between emotional and spiritual truths found through free-spirited interpretation of the Bible and the widely accepted assumptions of modern science and technology. If we use the Scripture as a screen against which we artistically project our own experiences of the soul, there is no need to declare its contents true or false according to the standards of verification that we use now in scientific or historical inquiry.

I treasure the Bible, even though I don't believe in it in an orthodox Christian manner. I find it full of glorious poetry, elegant mythology, profound spiritual insight, good common sense, sound precepts of morality and wise government, and fascinating historical accounts. It captivates me with the intrigue of figuring out who Jesus was, as the historic and mythic personality and as the divinity that he experienced in himself. Intimate as I am with this book, it continually amazes me—as it did in my encounter with Dirty Bill over the story of Jesus and the fig tree. It may not be the only authoritative and infallible word of God, but it is certainly the source of much of the language I use to talk about God.

10

Scripture and Freedom

He e-mailed me that familiar line: "I need to talk to you about some religious issues."

When we met, he told me his story. He had grown up in a church which taught that the Bible was inerrant—literally true and authoritative in every way. He was an exceptionally bright and curious high school student, but he never seriously questioned his church's doctrine.

He got accepted into Stanford, but his church friends warned him sternly about going to such a godless college. His answer was unassailable. "We have the truth, don't we? It stands up for itself, doesn't it?"

"Yes, of course," they replied.

"Then what do I have to worry about at Stanford? The truth is the truth, and I know it, so what can shake it?" Fearlessly, off he went to Stanford.

But it only took the first quarter of "Civ"—the humanities core curriculum—to blow out of the water his belief in absolute biblical authority. Shown the historical-critical method of reading texts such as the Bible, he could not deny that it contradicted his belief system. It threw him into a mortally serious crisis of faith, which led him to my door. Everything and everybody that mattered most to him had been directed by biblical authoritarianism. Giving it up would shatter his whole life, and cut him adrift from his family and closest community. I could see the devastating consequences for him of questioning the absolute authority of the Bible. So instead of contributing to the collapse of his cosmos, my main role was to sit and listen to him as he struggled.

His way of coping with this crisis was to embrace it with the full force of his prodigious intellect. He decided to major in religion. Voraciously, he consumed the writings of the greatest theologians, from Augustine through Aquinas, from Luther through Karl Barth. Every few months, I would meet with him and listen to his most recent theological ruminations. His parents could tell that he was drifting from the narrow way, so they forbade him to major in religion. He obeyed them and majored in history, but found a way to take religion classes to meet his history requirements.

This student was faced with a devastating choice: to violate the absolute biblical law of his family and church, or to violate the compelling conclusions of his intellect. Unfortunately, there are many Christians in America who seem serious about forcing that second choice upon all of us. They seek "Christian dominion"—a fundamentalist Christian society and government.

Ironically, a few hundred years ago biblical authoritarianism was a relatively progressive idea. The church had become a corrupt institution, and the people of Europe were clamoring for a civil society based on laws rather than on the whims of popes and princes. The Pope was the ruler of the church, but the Protestant reformers rejected him and made the Bible the ruler of their churches. At the time of the Reformation, the rigid authority of the Bible was a great step forward for the church, because it liberated Christians from a degenerated ecclesiastical hierarchy, and became the basis of the idea of the rule of the law rather than the rule of the prince. The authority of the Bible was the foundation of the emerging legal systems of the new democracies. But for several reasons, the Bible can no longer serve as the primary source of authority for church and society.

The pluralism of the United States and most other democracies is incompatible with a strictly Bible-centered social order. Converting the United States to a Christian theocracy would violate huge constituencies of nonbelievers and believers of other faiths, and tremendous social unrest would result. It is hard to imagine a governable United States existing as a fundamentalist Christian state.

While their dream is far-fetched and extreme, the motivation of fundamentalists is certainly understandable, rooted in what their faith tells them is right. People who believe that the Bible is the ultimate authority of their lives may find it hard to reconcile with and fit into the values of a secular, pluralistic society. It is easier to live under only one structure of authority—as long as that structure and authority are the ones that happen to govern your own personal beliefs.

Another reality troubling to some traditional Christians is that pluralistic secular culture can be corrosive to biblical fundamentalism. If the two are allowed to peacefully coexist forever, pluralism is likely to win out over worship of the Bible. The only way for fundamentalists to avoid losing that battle is to declare all-out war on secular pluralism. This is exactly what they have done.

But pluralism is healthy—even for Christianity. The government of the United States is never going to be a perfect reflection of my personal value system and religious assumptions, no matter how certain I may be about their ultimate correctness. Alternatives that challenge my beliefs are healthy. An America ruled by Scripture would not be good for Christians any more than it would be good for others. It would tend to fossilize Christianity, preventing it from evolving as it faces new challenges in a changing society.

If we embrace pluralism, we are implicitly turning away from the historic Christian claim that the Bible is the ultimate source of authority about how people should relate to God and each other. Little support for pluralism can be found in the Bible when it is read and applied in a fundamentalist manner. A literal, legalistic reading of the Scriptures will also yield the following odious conclusions: women are to be subservient to men in all aspects of life; non-Jews are inferior to Jews; Jews are responsible for their own persecution; slavery is acceptable; homosexuality is evil; and it is best to be celibate.

Theologically moderate or liberal Christians try to gloss over these difficulties by putting them in historical context, downplaying them in relation to other passages. But if we are going to pretend that the Bible is the ultimate foundation of the church, we aren't going to be able to ignore these blatantly racist, sexist, and homophobic passages. The fundamentalists are right in this regard: we have to choose one or the other— secular pluralism or biblical dominion. I choose pluralism, and reject the concept of the Bible as ultimate authority.

We may not understand or get along with them all the time, but if there were no practicing Buddhists or Muslims or adherents of Native American religions, Christians would be impoverished by their absence. We are joyful when it happens that they find their way to a Christian path. But not everyone need accept Jesus as their personal Lord and Savior and become conventional Christians. Something precious would be lost to the world if all Jews were for Jesus.

◈

There is an authority higher than Scripture: it is the Holy Spirit, the creative inspiration that comes from encounter with God. The Holy Spirit urges us toward justice and mercy, always pointing beyond existing social structures and religious institutions. The Holy Spirit makes room for new insights, for changes in moral codes, and for new expressions of spirituality. The Holy Spirit can't be contained only in the Bible, won't confine itself to the doctrines of the church, and won't enshrine itself in the Constitution. "The wind blows where it chooses," said Jesus, "and you hear the sound of it, but you do not know where it comes from or where it goes. So it is with everyone who is born of the Spirit." (John 3:8)

Changing the relationship of Christianity to the Bible, letting it be a limitless source of inspiration instead of a rigid authority code, is not going to happen because one group convinces another of the better way. It is going to happen when adherents of "religion" and seekers of "spirituality" quest together for a society where everybody has dignity, where there is vibrant community life, and where there is real political and economic democracy.

If the Holy Spirit can deliver a divine message to one person while another receives quite a different revelation, how do we sort out the question of spiritual authority? It is not enough to simply declare that each individual makes his or her own religion. Whether or not we're aware of it, we do depend upon sources of authority outside ourselves in matters of faith.

Since the colonial era, it has been a widespread assumption in American Protestant Christianity that individuals are competent to interpret the Bible for themselves. A related assumption, and one of the foundations of American citizenship, is that individual voters are competent not only to choose their leaders, but also to voluntarily create and sustain all the institutions of democracy.

A recent controversy in the Southern Baptist Convention illustrates how enduring this principle is. Conflict arose because the denominational leaders spelled out several theological and moral positions. A number of churches withdrew from the Convention as a result of this codification of Southern Baptist theology. The churches objected strenuously to being told what to think or how to act—even though they agreed with most of the principles that had been turned into official dogma! In their view, the Southern Baptist Convention had violated the more important principles of local church independence and freedom of the individual to follow his or her God-given conscience.

This independence of mind among lay people is hardly isolated to Protestants. Most of my Catholic friends tell me they are quite comfortable following those teachings of their church that they accept, and ignoring those that they cannot accept. They respect the authority of the Catholic Church up to a point; but in their hearts and by their actions, they recognize a higher authority.

It is typically American for individuals to sort out their religious beliefs on their own. From the old principle of individual empowerment to interpret the Bible, it is not that big a leap for Americans to say, as they do in increasing numbers today, "I don't need to belong to any church—I have my own personal religion."

The difficulty with taking this leap is that it obstructs a healthy dialogue about matters of the soul. If each of us has his or her own religion, how do we find a common language? If one's religion is entirely personal, can it rightly be called a religion at all? Our souls yearn to commune with each other, but this becomes hard without some kind of shared spiritual culture.

I am the minister of a small congregation that has a very simple structure and an unusually open theology. But our church still needs a system of authority, some criteria for determining what constitutes a meaningful worship service. It may not be written down, it may not be codified, and it may not be fixed forever, but we do have an evolving tradition that has become normative in shaping our Sunday service. We have consistent habits of doing business to allow our members to participate meaningfully in decision making. These become authoritative practices for maintaining our church as an institution. A little structure can go a long way to keep a church together. Keeping the church as simple as possible helps to avoid the effects that give the word "authority" a negative connotation.

I recently preached a sermon in which I emphatically professed that the soul does not know the difference between thinking about doing something and actually doing it. I was expounding on Jesus' teaching about the law when he said that anger was just as bad as murder, and that lust was just as bad as adultery (Matthew 5). After worship, two of our members came up to me at coffee hour and said I had gone too far.

"The soul *does* know the difference," they said. "You exaggerated!" We had a brief but lively exchange about the distinctions among soul, mind, and emotions.

Both these people have been faithful church members for many years. I respect them and they respect me. All three of us implicitly recognized that while we must finally answer to the Holy Spirit in our own consciences, we still need to grapple with issues of faith together. We need to honor our common religious language, honor what has been handed down to us through Scripture and tradition, honor each other's experiences, and honor the process of spiritual exploration exemplified by our discussion at coffee hour. As the preacher, mine was not the final authoritative word on the subject. But my role as preacher is part of a system of spiritual authority that makes a meaningful communal religious life possible. Supporting this system of authority does not imply that everything it delivers ought to be accepted blindly. On the contrary, it maintains a healthy community in which the authority of the Holy Spirit in every individual heart can find fullest expression.

◇

The world is now witnessing the emergence of a global culture. Whether we like it or not, there is a very rapid convergence of thought, language, and behavior around the planet. Perhaps because we see things more and more through the lens of planetary citizenship, the world at the same time appears more disturbingly fractious and sectarian than ever. Tiny ethnic groups strive mightily for recognition or autonomy within larger nation-states. Religious groups flaunt their identities more than ever, even to the point of inciting armed conflicts. As televisions, cell phones, and Internet connections proliferate, so also do the reactions of sects and ethnic groups against the homogenization of the human family. The exaggerated truth-claims of dogmatic Christian groups—and dogmatic non-Christian groups—are symptoms of the stresses that come with globalization.

And there are very good reasons why ethnic and religious groups feel threatened by this trend. The precious particularities of these cultures are faced with annihilation by video games, Hollywood action films, and fast-food chains. Their unique spiritual insights are threatened with what is perceived to be the shallow worldview of capitalism and consumerism.

There *is* a way to live in two worlds at once. There is a way to live in the global context and in an ethnically or religiously specific context at the same time. Indeed, one makes the other possible.

To commune with each other, we need to honor the validity of each other's specific cultural backgrounds as we do our own. Without our particularities, there would be little ground for interesting discourse, because there wouldn't be anything new to say! We need to continue to practice our different religions while having a deep level of respect for other belief systems. By abandoning the chauvinism that claims one or another religion is supreme, people can practice the best parts of our diverse religious heritage while being profoundly enriched by a global spiritual culture. The authority structure of each historic religion has its place, but there is a higher authority, a Holy Spirit that enables practitioners of all religions to commune with each other in "sighs too deep for words." (Romans 8:26)

"However different the paths followed by different civilizations, we can find the same basic message at the core of most religions and cultures throughout history: people should revere God as a phenomenon that transcends them; they should revere one another; and they should not harm their fellow humans. To my mind, reflecting on this message is the only way out of the crisis the world finds itself in today." These words of Vaclav Havel, president of the Czech Republic and hero of the struggle against communist totalitarianism in his country, point to the emergence of a global culture that finds a common language of spirituality. They come from a man who is not a professing member of any faith, yet understands the profound need for the whole human race to walk humbly before God.

PART IV

Open Christianity and the Hard Questions

11

Death, Resurrection, and Eternal Life

Many of the drug addicts we served when I was director of the Urban Ministry were infected with HIV. One of them, Buck, experienced a spiritual resurrection during the last year of his physical life. We discovered he had AIDS when he came to the drop-in center one morning and couldn't talk. I had assumed he had lost so much weight because of his addiction to crack cocaine. But when Jeanne Toal, our caseworker, rushed him to the hospital she overheard a nurse mention that Buck was HIV-positive. Later we learned that he had temporarily lost his speech because of an AIDS-related lesion in his brain.

Jeanne helped him find housing and other social services when he was released from the hospital, and spent many hours with him offering spiritual and emotional support. His little skid-row room became a haven of acceptance and loving hospitality in the chaotic single-room occupancy hotel where he lived. The other residents loved to go to his room because it was peaceful there.

Buck had been a big, fat, bearded biker and dope dealer. Now he was a skinny guy with a radiant smile. In the dying process his ego passed away, leaving only the love that is Christ to shine through. In the months before his death, he was reunited with many members of his family, reconciling with them years after his own bad choices had estranged them from him.

One after another AIDS-related disorder weakened him. An hour or two before he died, Jeanne, sitting at his bedside, recorded his last words uttered in a semiconscious state:

> "Let me go.
> Let it go.
> Let me go.
> Let me know.
>
> He knows.
> He always lets me go.
> Let me go now.
>
> It works.
> I'm really sure.
> It works
> Like that.
>
> Um hm. Um hm.
> Um hm. Yeah.
>
> It's quiet.
> Awfully quiet.
> I need to go.
> I'm scared.
> It's okay.
> Do it now,
> Right now.

Let me go for it.
Let it go.
Let it go instead.
Let it scare.

Everybody's scared of that place.
Let's go.
They're scared all the time.
Why?
I don't know.
Let it show.

They say let it go.
The skull.
They don't know.

I've got to go.
We'd better go.
Let's go.

Children make me smile.
They always let me go.
They always let me in there.
They let it go.

It's going.
It makes sense.

All right!
I love it.
Let's go!"

Where did Buck go? What happens after we die?

The Old Testament presents no clear belief system about salvation or damnation in an afterlife. It appears that the early Jews did not believe in the traditional Christian heaven and hell. Life happened while they were alive, and when they died, that was the end. Anything like salvation was something people experienced during their natural lives.

But the Jewish patriarchs took burial very seriously (Genesis chapters 23 and 48). The ancients (and indigenous cultures all over the world today) did not make the same distinctions between the animate and the inanimate that we do. If you assume everything is in some way alive, including rocks and water and air, it is not much of a leap to believe that there is power in the dry bones of your ancestors. Reclaiming for ourselves this ancient awareness of the life-force in all things could go far in relieving our modern anxieties about death.

By New Testament times, the Jewish people were influenced by the ideas of the Greek culture, with its myths about the afterlife. Jesus himself expressed inconsistent descriptions of what happens at physical death. In one passage, he talked about what is translated in English as "hell" (Matthew 18:9), but the original Greek word was *Gehenna*, a valley just outside Jerusalem which served as a constantly burning garbage dump. At other points, he talked about heaven and hell in a more Greek fashion, suggesting there was a place of eternal reward for the saved, and another place of eternal punishment for the wicked and the unbelievers (Luke 16:19-31).

The traditional Christian descriptions of heaven and hell are not clearly delineated in the Bible. They are a composite of ancient Greek and Near Eastern folk traditions, various biblical stories from the Old and New Testaments, and images that continued to be developed into the Middle Ages. Over the millennia in the Judeo-Christian tradition, the concept of salvation evolved from a spiritual state of reconciliation with God while one is alive, into inclusion of physical rescue from the sufferings of the earth and the torments of the underworld.

If, indeed, Jesus meant that those who didn't believe in him would be damned to roast in hellfire for eternity, then I would have to reject this part of his teaching. But the Jesus of my faith demonstrated that salvation was the spiritual state of being at one with God—something he and his followers experienced in their natural lifetimes. "The kingdom of heaven is among (or within) you," he taught (Luke 17:21). For him, damnation was the spiritual state of separation from God, something he and his followers also experienced in their earthly lives. After all, in his agony on the cross, Jesus said, "My God, my God, why have you forsaken me?" (Matthew 27:46)   That was hell—a familiar experience for anyone who has endured terrible suffering or loss.

The early Christians believed that Christ had come to bring heaven down to earth. The ancients believed that the cosmos was hierarchical: God ruled the outermost sphere of the universe, and successive levels of subordinate power ruled those spheres below them. In biblical times, kingdoms were much different from the nation-states of today. They were not defined exclusively by geography and contiguous boundaries on maps. A kingdom consisted of everyone who was loyal to a particular king. If you pledged loyalty to that king, then you were part of that kingdom. One of the most radical teachings of the early Christians was the idea that God had come down to rule the earth directly, bypassing the "powers and principalities" of the lower heavens. God, through the coming of the Christ, had come into the world in person, and now the kingdom of heaven on earth was in the process of coming into being.

Since most kings of the ancient world claimed that their power was delegated to them in some way by God or the gods, the Judeo-Christian idea of pledging direct loyalty to God as one's only king was considered seditious. The political system of the ancient world was viewed as a manifestation of the cosmic order, so the early Christians' revolutionary cosmology had profound practical consequences. Through mystical union with the divine, you pledged your loyalty to God and entered the kingdom of heaven on earth. That is why Jesus would tell people that they were close to or far from God's kingdom: they were more or less awake to the fact that God's kingdom was among them already, more or less ready to take the radical step of abandoning loyalty to the kings of this world.

Jesus' many sayings about "the kingdom of heaven" imply this new intimacy between sky and ground, between God and people. Jesus was not talking about an afterlife so much as he was describing a future life that would happen as more and more people became "subjects" of God alone, in their hearts and through their actions. God and humanity were working together to make heaven and earth into one. "The glory that you have given me I have given them, so that they may be one, as we are one . . ." (John 17:22)   This communion between humanity and God would revolutionize the world with social justice and peace.

Salvation and damnation, heaven and hell, are experiences that people have during their natural lifetimes here on earth. But I still take the idea of an "afterlife" seriously. I have watched people die, and I have read and heard accounts of people who have been revived after being pronounced clinically dead. It seems to me that it is impossible for a person to experience his or her own death. You can experience near-death, those last few seconds or microseconds of brain activity that appear to last past the cessation of detectable heart or brain activity. But no one can experience the end of life; when it is over, you aren't there to experience it. Therefore, from the point of view of the person who is dying, life may be eternal, without end.

Some people who have been brought back from near-death report a profoundly beautiful experience as their bodies stop functioning, an experience that continues to unfold and does not suggest an imminent cessation of the experience. Others who have been brought back from near-death don't remember anything at all—including any experience of being "dead." For them, it was like waking up from a dreamless sleep. So death as the end, the cessation of subjective experience, is not something we ever know. We can only know life. And in some cases, it appears that life takes on an eternal, endless quality during the last minutes or seconds of bodily functioning.

Eternal life is a subjective experience. From the point of view of the people watching somebody die, that person's existence comes to a final end. But from the point of view of the person dying, his or her life is without end. Part of that experience of eternal life may be frightening and painful. But sometimes that subjective experience of eternal life resembles the traditional Christian vision of what heaven is like.

I don't think we have total control over our experience of eternal life at death. However, I suspect we can prepare ourselves for it by practicing self-awareness, letting go of negative thoughts, and ceasing to cling so tightly to our bodies, possessions, and egos.

One of the most important things I have discovered from practicing prayerful meditation and other spiritual disciplines is that much of what I think and feel is *optional*. Now, pain itself is not usually optional. We all go through pain. Bad things happen beyond our control. But how we interpret this pain, how we think about it, how we react to it—all this is optional. These are things we can change. Making the change may not be easy, but it is certainly possible.

Hell is the most negative imaginable interpretation of what life and the universe are all about. But it's an *optional* interpretation. We really do have the choice of experiencing that same life and that same universe as heaven. Jesus was not in denial about the existence of the Roman Empire and its oppression of the people of Israel. But in the same place and among the same people of the Roman Empire, he saw the kingdom of heaven on earth. Everywhere he went, everywhere he looked, he found evidence of its existence. He chose to interpret the world around him in a positive and hopeful way, and his vision changed the world both spiritually and physically.

Jesus saw that the Roman Empire existed, but it was not the only reality in the world—he exercised his option to see many other realities and possibilities. Likewise, we can recognize that while today's world has some characteristics of a global empire with a serious compassion deficit, there are other options. We can look around and see signs of the coming of the kingdom of heaven, inspiring us to create a more humane social order.

The Tibetan Buddhist sages understood this optional quality of reality. *The Tibetan Book of the Dead* is a guide to the soul as it passes through the experiences of eternal life at physical death. Each chapter is the soul's encounter with a different dreadful demon, and each chapter ends with an admonition to the soul to recognize that the demons are optional interpretations, that the soul can move on and experience the process of eternal life in a positive way. This is excellent advice for living as well as for dying.

There are nights when I wake up in the middle of a terrible dream, and it takes a long time to remember that absolutely everything in it is optional. I can take that dream gun out of the hands of the dream bad guy and turn it into a dream paintbrush and paint a glorious dream desert sunset and then dream-walk into that sunset, if I choose. But in the midst of the dream, I forget that I have such a choice between hell and heaven. I'm too busy clutching my idea of what I am.

In the midst of everyday life, I forget that I have a choice about how to react when a guy in a big red pickup truck thunders around my car, cuts me off at a freeway off-ramp, and forces me to stand on my brake pedal. I can interpret that incident as an outrageous insult to my person, a gross violation of propriety worthy of my righteous wrath, and an appropriate time for the use of angry hand and finger gestures. Or I can experience it as just another of those common things that happens when I drive my car, no different from slowing down at an intersection or dodging a piece of wood lying on the roadway as I daydream of more pleasant things. One interpretation is no more or less "correct" than the other. But one lands me in hell, and the other in heaven. I get to choose between them.

Salvation is the positive interpretation of life and the universe: choosing bliss instead of torment, recognizing that since my real Self is one with God, who is eternal, I don't need to cling so desperately to my body or to my ego. This is the salvation that Jesus offered as he reminded his followers not to worry, not to clutch after transitory things, not to fear the loss of the body when the soul is eternal. This is the salvation he offered when he reminded his disciples that "the kingdom of heaven is among you." It is already available in this imperfect, sometimes painful life. Am I saved? Yes, sometimes. Am I damned? Yes, sometimes. But Jesus gave me the good news that I have a choice between the two, throughout life and even through death.

Even in his final minutes, Buck knew he had a choice, and he made a decision: *"Let's go!"*

It wasn't until Buck's memorial service that his family came together. Their mutual mistrust and hatred had kept them apart for over 20 years.

Our tradition of conducting memorial services for homeless people was to get everyone into a circle—homeless folks, family members, Urban Ministry staff and volunteers—and pass around a loaf of bread. As the bread passed from hand to hand, people in the circle took their piece and said their piece, sharing stories or thoughts about the person who had died. When we started Buck's memorial service, the comments of his family members were strained and polite, but as the bread moved around the circle, people became more honest. Their hearts opened with love for the man who had died, and for each other. By the time the bread returned to me the circle was erupting with tears and laughter. I witnessed the miracle of a family coming back to life after being entombed for two decades.

◈

I know Jesus as a mortal human being, not a being of a different order from the rest of us. But while I don't accept the myth of his resurrection as factual truth, it is certainly the most important "soul truth" of Christianity. Jesus died, but the Christ, his true divine Self, conquered death and lives. When I experience mystical union with God in meditation, my ego dies, and the Christ is resurrected within and through me. Resurrection is something I have witnessed many times in my own life and in the lives of others around me.

The New Testament is ambiguous about the nature of the resurrection. The gospels and the Book of Acts emphasize that Jesus physically rose from the dead (John 20:24-29). But in his letters, St. Paul makes it clear that he believed the resurrection was strictly spiritual (1 Corinthians 15:44). *The fact that these two very different perspectives exist side by side in the Bible is a sign, ignored by many Christians, that there ought to be room in the church for differing interpretations.* But whatever the outcome of this contradiction, the soul truth of the resurrection can be seen in moments like the memorial service of Buck, the man who died of AIDS.

The soul truth of the resurrection is evident in the story from the gospel of Luke in which some of Jesus' followers were walking from Jerusalem down to the town of Emmaus (Luke 24:13-35). There were reports that Jesus had risen from the dead. His followers were talking about all that had happened as they walked down the road. A stranger came along and asked them what they were discussing. They told him, and then he went on to interpret the Jesus story in terms of Old Testament prophecy. When they got to Emmaus, the followers invited him to eat with them, and asked him to bless the bread. When he did so, they recognized him as Jesus, and in that same instant, he disappeared. Afterward, the followers said, "Were not our hearts burning within us while he was talking to us on the road, while he was opening the Scriptures to us?" The story ends with this punch line: ". . . he had been made known to them in the breaking of the bread." Whenever we walk together down another road, and get together to take our piece and share our piece, the resurrected Christ can become known, making our hearts burn within us.

We need to get past the debate about whether or not Jesus physically rose from the dead. It is a useless exercise, a trivial pursuit, compared to the opportunity we have to experience the soul-truth of the resurrection.

Grief itself is resurrection. At the loss of someone we love, we are overwhelmed—possessed, really—by a life-force that is often beyond our conscious control. Waves of emotion surface unannounced; tears flow for no immediate reason. When somebody close to us dies, or when a precious relationship ends, it is as if a new kind of life rises from the dead inside us and takes us over for a while.

Once I got a phone call from a woman who wanted to volunteer at the Urban Ministry's Christmas dinner for the homeless and hungry. I recited my usual spiel: "I'm sorry to tell you that we have all the volunteers we need for Christmas—we sign them up in November. But you can come to the meal anyway; the whole community is invited. And we need volunteer help the rest of the year . . ." She was one of hundreds of people who wanted to help on the same day, Christmas. On that one day we got many times more volunteers than the number of homeless we fed on an average day! It was frustrating for us at the Urban Ministry to deal with this onslaught of people calling to volunteer on the same day. We set up our Christmas meal so that it would serve the homeless and housed alike, because we had learned that many people volunteer at Christmas to counteract their desperate feelings of loneliness during the holidays. They needed to join us at Christmas, for their own reasons, as much as the people of the streets did.

The woman on the phone said she'd be glad to come to the meal, and that she'd bring a casserole to share. But she went further. "I need to be at the Christmas meal. I need to volunteer after Christmas, too. My husband died this past year, and I am not doing very well. I have not adjusted. I need to get out and get involved with people."

I was moved by her story. "All of us have a need, or we wouldn't be here," I answered. "I have a need, our volunteers have a need, and homeless people have a need to be part of the Urban Ministry. I'm glad you need to do this; it's a qualification for working here. When can you start?" After Christmas, she began coming to work with us every week. Volunteering was part of her own "raising from the death" of her husband, a visible demonstration of the soul-truth in the gospel resurrection story.

12

A New Story
of the Universe

One night, I was station-surfing as I drove my car. I paused when I caught a radio preacher explaining why the earth's exposed strata and fossils appear to be millions of years old, when the Bible tells us that the earth was created only about 6,000 years ago. "You know that furniture they sell—they call it 'distressed'? It is new furniture, but it has been artificially given the appearance of age. Well, that is what the Lord has done to the earth. He has given it the appearance of great age . . ." And so on.

I couldn't help but ask myself: what sort of God likes cheap furniture?

Matters of life, death, and life beyond death invite us to ponder hard questions about the relationship of the realm of the spiritual and the realm of the physical. Are they different manifestations of the same reality, are they distinctly separate, or do they intersect somehow? How can science and religion inform each other, if at all?

Understanding the creation and evolution of the universe is not just the business of science. It is an imperative for the human soul. A literal reading of the creation story in Genesis strains the credulity of any reason-loving mind. But what alternative is there to satisfy the heart's craving to know its place in the grand order of the universe?

Because I have encountered God in and through all sorts of people and things, I have a hunch that God is to be found everywhere in the cosmos; that God is the source, essence, and goal of all that exists. I have a powerful urge to integrate my spiritual experience with my understanding of how the universe works. And while I don't have all the answers, I do have faith that there is an important connection between science and religion.

My spiritual experience urges me to seek a unified theory of everything—a meaningful response to the question of why and how the universe came into existence, how it functions, and where it is headed. My spiritual practice leaves me with the conviction that such a whole exists, even if I don't know exactly how all things are integrated into it.

Traditional religions provide (or imply) cosmologies, which are systems that fit—or try to fit—all things into one meaningful unity. But Christian cosmology has fallen apart. The cosmology of the first-century Christians who wrote the New Testament is radically different from that of even the most orthodox Christians of today. The questions and answers posed by that radio evangelist are ones that would never have entered the minds of people during the New Testament era. Neither biblical nor current traditional Christianity squares with what science has to tell us about the way the universe works.

And on the other side, science alone is not sufficient to provide a unified theory of everything. It can tell us that the Big Bang started the universe, but it can't tell us why it happened. Science can't answer the question of the universe's meaning and purpose, yet any cosmic story of the origin and direction of the universe must be compatible with science's best theories. How do we reconcile the yearnings of our hearts with the disciplined observations of our sciences to compose a new and satisfying cosmology?

◈

The shadowed swell of the moon was dimly lit by the bright backside of the earth, on whose darkening side I stood in the Anza-Borrego Desert of southern California. I faced into a rush of cool air that fell from the steep, stony mountains above the campground where I had gone on a sojourn of solitude. Yet my body was still warmed by the radiant heat stored in the earth at my feet, as I stared at the crescent of the moon nestled voluptuously against its dimly lit lover. Round, dressed into shape by the laws of physics; to look at that crescent moon was to stare, unabashed, at the curvaceousness of space-time.

That the moon and the earth are spheres has been common knowledge for hundreds of years, but I am not used to it yet. Despite our intellectual assent to the contrary, we so often talk as though the earth were flat and the moon an illuminated gem on the smooth crystal vault of heaven. If the moon is continually congealed out of the gravitational curvature of the universe, still struck by stray meteorites, how can it be "full"? How can it be "new," pitted as it is with the ancient pockmarks of the matter it sucked into itself? There is no "quarter" of a spherical moon, no literal wedge of a ball that big.

What is the true story of the cosmos? And the best poem for the moon?

Our need for a new cosmology is amply demonstrated by the fact that, after all these years, the theory of evolution is still up for debate in America. Anyone who drives an automobile has been a witness to the battle of the fish ornaments on the rear ends of cars. The metal fish ornament began as a copy of the secret sign that marked the presence of early Christians hiding in the catacombs under the city of Rome. The word ICTHUS meant "fish," but it also was an acronym for the Greek words for "Jesus Christ, Son of God, Savior." At some point, a strident defender of the theory of evolution—perhaps unfairly characterizing all Christians as creationists—came up with a rival ornament that put the name DARWIN inside the fish. Next came the fish with the name JESUS inside. Then the DARWIN fish sprouted legs. Then the anti-evolutionists came up with a big JESUS fish that eats the DARWIN fish. Every so often, the logos evolve further, adding new details as they compete in the fish-eat-fish world of public opinion.

There is good reason for the tenuous status of the theory of evolution in the hearts and minds of the public. Science has pretty well established that evolution happens through natural selection, but it can't tell us exactly how it happens, and not always why it happens. And there is a mystery in the study of evolution: it appears that organisms sometimes evolve in "quantum" fashion. Whole new organs and body parts appear suddenly in the fossil record. Natural selection of random mutations can account for changes in the finer details of an organ, but can't always explain the sudden emergence of a new organ or feature. It seems that too many random mutations would have to occur at once for an animal to suddenly evolve a wing out of a leg, for example. Perhaps some other evolutionary process is at work, or we would find more intermediate forms in the fossil record. Perhaps something is driving organisms to leap and fly from one level of complexity to the next, sometimes with no obvious steps in between.

Science investigates the chain of causes and effects that moves from the past into the present, resulting in the phenomena we observe around us. But while there are certainly "root" causes for the things we see, there may also be "leaf" causes that science does not address. The universe may be as attracted by the pull of its future as it is pushed by the causes and effects of its past.

Is there a "leaf" cause moving the cosmos to evolve into more complex forms of matter and energy, and into more complex levels of consciousness? What is this tendency that has driven the universe to congeal atoms out of the primordial soup? And molecules out of atoms? And living cells out of molecules? And organs and organisms out of living cells? And minds, or spirits, out of brains? Each new level is a quantum leap that cannot necessarily be explained by reduction to its constituent parts.

It is here that traditional Christianity argues for the existence of a divine Creator. Since science has not found the missing links of biological or cosmic evolution from one form to another, the argument goes, there must be a God who miraculously creates things—sometimes out of nothing, sometimes out of what God has already created. But few scientists find this to be a compelling line of reasoning. There have been many mysteries in the course of scientific exploration, and repeatedly those voids have been filled with sound scientific explanations, eliminating the need for a miracle-working "God of the gaps." The fact that evolution often seems to occur in quantum leaps with no intermediate steps may not be evidence of God's creative agency, but rather of the incomplete knowledge of scientists. Scientists continue to probe for missing links in intermediate fossils, for missing links in their theories, and for alternative theories to account for such phenomena.

The eclipse of the "God of the gaps" began to accelerate with the remarkable discoveries of Sir Isaac Newton. Newton was as much a theologian as a scientist. He did not question whether or not the Bible was true; he only questioned *how* it was true. He believed that God had created nature with a set of orderly rules, and sought to describe them. But he also believed

God could change the rules whenever and however God saw fit. The miracles of the Bible were, in Newton's argument, really miraculous: divine interventions that violated the divine laws. But Newton's belief in a supernatural God who intervened willfully in creation was threatened by the very force of his argument that nature was orderly and predictable. Belief in God as creator and shaper of the universe was a victim of Newton's scientific success—which, ironically, was inspired by his religious impulse. After Newton's lifetime, as scientists and engineers exploited his discoveries of the laws of nature, the existence of God became less and less necessary as an assumption.

Of course, more recently Newton's laws have been challenged by relativity and then by quantum mechanics. The current view of the physical world is of a mutable cosmic order, governed not by a predictable Newtonian clockwork set in motion by a remote God, but by a system of uncertainties described by statistics. Some of the features of the quantum conception of the universe are so strange in light of Newton's world view that biblical miracles seem tame by comparison. Quantum mechanics boggles the minds of scientists more than the traditional Christian claim that Jesus really could walk on water.

The divorce of God from science has disenchanted Western civilization. Our sense of mystery, of awe, of wonder toward the natural world has no place in the formal culture of science and technology, even though individual scientists are often privately subject to these experiences. Our souls are impoverished by this cultural marginalization of our aesthetic and spiritual sensitivities.

This is especially evident at the universities, where relatively few resources go to scholars in the humanities. Universities originally were focused on the study of the universe as a whole. A generally accepted cosmology intimately connected all fields of study together. But the universities of today function in almost exactly the opposite manner. Since the wider culture has no coherent cosmology, the university has devolved into a loose federation of scholars in isolated fields of study that share no common universe. The result is a trivialization of many scholarly pursuits.

Physicists have been tantalized for years by the possibility of discovering the "unified field theory" which would account for all forms of matter and energy in the universe, and would explain its origin and destiny. Various candidate theories have been offered, but none has yet gained a consensus. I, too, am excited by the prospect that such a theory may someday be found, making a "universe" out of our current "multiverse." If and when it is discovered, it may take a mathematical form. Perhaps this mathematical construct will be translatable into a mythic, poetic story . . . a new Genesis.

Mathematics is not just the language of physics; in a way, it is the very essence of what physicists study. The number "one," for instance, is a universal idea. We use it in many ways, in many contexts. We symbolize it with various mathematical or linguistic notations. But the underlying idea of the number "one" remains the same no matter how or when or where it is used. It doesn't have different personalities in different contexts. There is only one number "one."

In the same manner, subatomic particles—the entities that exist in the realm of quantum physics—don't have different personalities in different contexts. Electrons taken as a group are not like, say, red 1967 Volkswagen Beetles taken as a group. While they were mass produced and intended to be identical, each red 1967 VW sedan is slightly different from the next. There were minute variations among them even when they first came off the assembly line, and further differences are apparent after decades of use. But every electron is absolutely identical to every other electron. It could even be said that there are no "electrons," there are only many instances of the one phenomenon called "electron." The electron is the same sort of thing as the number "one"; neither of them is made out of constituent parts that could give instances of them any individuality. It has been observed that subatomic physical reality is the same thing as the mathematical ideas that describe it!

Because we live in a culture that makes a clear distinction between symbol and reality, between words and the things to which they refer, it is difficult for us to comprehend that in a way, mathematics and physical reality are one and the same. But our religious heritage can help us with this difficulty. In Christianity, we have the myth that the bread and wine of the Mass are the actual body and blood of Jesus. These symbols of the presence of God are traditionally considered to be the same as that to which they refer. Likewise, in the Judeo-Christian tradition (as well as in other religions), the name of God is holy because it is not just a symbol: the name of God *is* God.

So when we find the "unified field theory," I suspect that it will be an idea which shares the reality of that to which it refers.

But what is the nature of our minds, which have such ideas? We know that our brains are electrochemical systems. Electrons are exchanged across nerve membranes, and these electrical impulses firing in neural networks result in the brain activity associated with our thoughts. One noted mathematician, Roger Penrose, is tantalized by the possibility that the brain may also function at the quantum level: interactions of events and particles smaller than the atom may also be involved in our thought processes. If this is the case, our mathematical ideas may be one and the same as the minds we use to think them!

Quantum mechanics, which is now the foundation of our theories about the physical universe, points towards a profound intimacy between the observer and the observed, the thinker and the thought, the idea and that to which the idea refers. This sort of thinking is very much like that of the ancient mystical traditions of the religions of the world. It holds the hope of a re-enchantment, a re-union, of science and spirituality in which each will remain distinct, but will fit together in a coherent view of the universe. These words of Meister Eckhart, the fourteenth-century mystical Christian priest, begin to ring true once again: "The eye by which I see God is the eye by which God sees me. My eye and God's eye are one and the same—one in seeing, one in knowing, and one in loving." We are on the verge of divine communion with the universe: we are seeking an idea of the cosmos that will be of the same substance as the cosmos itself.

◇

Here is my contribution to the composition of a fresh story of the universe:

> The universe begins in a state of unity, like a meditative prayer in which there is no distinction between one's Self and God. From this initial quantum condition, the universe bursts forth and evolves. Subatomic particles emerge after the Big Bang— which might better be called the Creative Ecstasy—to make atoms, which then cool off to make molecules, which then cool off to make life forms, which then evolve into more and more complex life forms with brains, and then minds which gain consciousness of God. Our minds express themselves through more complex and subtle forms of society, and a global culture emerges. Scientific progress, artistic creativity, and social development are means by which human beings come to a deeper communion with divinity. The increasing exercise of justice with compassion tempers the innate destructive tendencies in all created things, signifying that the cosmos is moving toward the fulfillment of its divine nature. This universe continues to unfold on both a local and a cosmic scale. While many steps are taken backward, even more are taken forward in the direction of divine fulfillment. The ultimate end of this process may be what cosmologists call the Big Crunch,

*but might better be called the Divine Reunion, when the
universe returns to the unified state that existed before it
emerged.*

*Humanity and any life forms that may exist on other
worlds are the means by which the universe, which is God,
discovers and delights in itself and returns to itself to fulfill
its purpose. The life of the individual human being is a
microcosm: from conception, each person's development
mimics the evolutionary process of the universe. The individual
develops to the point of gaining adult consciousness and
awakening to the divine nature it shares with the rest of the
universe. This development can continue, heightening the
person's awareness of the presence of God in all things.
Thoughts and actions can become increasingly motivated by
the meaning, value, and purpose that the person shares with
the cosmos.*

◇

There is much in traditional Christianity that points toward
this cosmology. The Genesis story of creation is an inaccurate
natural history of the earth, but it expresses insights that are
still valid today. One of the two conflicting accounts of the creation in Genesis suggests that the creation happened in stages
that might be called an evolutionary process. From the primordial formless void, God formed the basic elements of light
and darkness, water and earth, then sea creatures, then land
creatures, and ultimately human beings. In the Garden of
Eden, human beings evolve to attain a God-like consciousness. In broad outline, taken figuratively, this story is not in
total conflict with scientific understanding of the origins of the
universe.

The New Testament implies a cosmology that is in some respects consistent with a modern view of the universe. In outline, the New Testament says the coming of Christ on earth resulted in a fundamental change in the cosmic order. In the New Testament era, most people believed that the universe was a series of layers: the seven heavens, which were concentric circles around the earth, each of the first six corresponding to a different heavenly body. Each one in ascending order had a higher spiritual value or more purely divine influence. St. Paul spoke of three heavens (2 Corinthians 12:2), which was a different expression of the same idea. The first heaven was the one between earth and the lowest shell of the seven heavens; the second consisted of the shells of the six heavenly bodies; and the third heaven was the same as "seventh heaven"—the realm of God.

First-century people generally believed that God ruled the cosmos in a hierarchical manner: God gave orders to the sixth heaven, which transmitted them to the fifth, and so on down through the layers until the divine will was expressed in imperfect form on earth. Essentially, their cosmos was a model of the Roman Empire, in which the Emperor did not rule directly, but through his vassal princes and their subordinates. The New Testament reveals that the early Christians believed Jesus broke through the seven heavens to bring the direct, personal reign of God to earth. They believed that his birth, ministry, and death changed the very nature of the cosmos.

Because few modern people begin with the assumption that the earth is the center of the universe and that there are seven heavens above it, this aspect of biblical cosmology doesn't make much sense to us. But to first-century Mediterranean people, Christian cosmology was a very progressive concept. It introduced the spiritually and politically radical idea that a normal human being, a commoner, could directly experience the pure presence of God, and discover for him or herself the will of God for his or her life. Because of this direct revelation of God, the world would never be the same; it would begin the process of fulfilling its purpose. This was an exalted view of the place of human beings in the cosmos, and a glorious vision of the purpose of the universe.

The new cosmology makes contemporary sense of this ancient Christian story. The Christian gospel is a myth that describes the evolution of awareness of God—the self-consciousness of the universe—that emerges in human beings. Instead of experiencing God as a vague, inaccessible deity on the other side of the sky, the early Christians discovered that God was immediately and personally present to them, experienced vividly in the here-and-now. This discovery led to an explosion of unconditional love, manifested in the work of Jesus and in the compassion that was evident in the lives of early Christians.

It is no accident that the Christian myth emerged within a few hundred years of other great world religions. I think it can be said that, indeed, our corner of the cosmos underwent a quantum leap of development in the relatively short time between the birth of the Buddha and the emergence of Islam. Traditional Christian cosmology contains this deep and enduring insight: the emergence of divine consciousness among human beings was an event of enormous significance for the universe.

So there is an alternative to traditional Christian cosmology and the dis-enchantment of modern science. It is to realize that when we learn more through science and technology, we are learning more about God. To understand God as the beginning, process, and ultimate end of the universe does not contradict anything that science has to say about the cosmos. It is a recognition that our personal spiritual experience of God unites us with the universe as a whole. God doesn't stand outside the universe, working miracles that defy the natural order, because God is manifested in and through the natural world. The universe came from something and is going somewhere, and our human consciousness of divinity is a critical turning point in its natural history. We always have more to learn about God than we know today, and part of this knowledge can only come through the rigorous practices of science.

We can't use Scripture to sort out the origin of species, and we can't use science to find the meaning and purpose of our lives. Science and religion need to remain separate disciplines. The key to success is for the two to maintain an intimate dialogue with each other.

◈

God is the principle or process by which the universe continues to be created. When I meditate, I experience this creativity: I move from a lower to a higher level of consciousness. The impulse that moves me out of experiencing myself in limited, mortal ways and toward an awareness of the boundless true Self—this tendency is God, and it is the same tendency that drives the universe to unfold its awesome marvels. Our urge to connect with those marvels is not just the fuzzy-headed response of dreamy poets or artists; it is our resonance with an enchantment integral to the universe itself.

The hoary-headed Creator on the Sistine Chapel ceiling is a picture that is hard to shake from Christian consciousness. But in order to honor the enduring Judeo-Christian insight that creation is a divine process, we cannot limit our cosmological vision to this image. The idea that God is an all-powerful entity that exists outside the universe, manipulating it directly or indirectly from a remote position, contradicts my own encounter with God within myself, and is not compatible with scientific understanding. But recognizing that the evolutionary process is divine does not contradict scientific theories of cosmic origins, either.

As for the dueling fish logos, I hope they will soon become extinct and disappear from the rear ends of automobiles, making way for the integration of serious science with our soulful yearning for meaning and purpose.

13

Good, Evil, and
the Will of God

*My arms held the baby swaddled lovingly in a soft blanket, but he
wasn't there. He had left his body behind, and had left his
shattered parents, members of our church, sitting next to me,
grieving the loss of all they had hoped for him during his short and
difficult life. His body had too many deformities. At the age of 10
weeks he lost the strength to withstand all the surgeries that were
necessary to give him a chance at life. One question haunted us as
we sat in that quiet room in the children's hospital: Why?*

What is the will of God? Can it be reconciled with suffering
and death? What way of life, what kind of society, does God
will for us?

Traditional Christianity claims to have a rather detailed
understanding of God's will for our lives. Among other things,
it tells us that God wants all people to be Christians, that God
wants us to be heterosexuals, that God wants us to belong to
certain churches and not others, and that God wants women
and men to have certain prescribed roles in family life. But the

belief that we can know God's will with certainty is not just confined to conservative Christians. For example, traditional Christians on the political left use the same language to assert that God wants particular forms of peace and social justice, or to say that it is God's will that homosexuals should be allowed to serve as ordained ministers.

All of these claims rest on the assumption that God's will isn't reflected in the realities that surround us. Traditional Christianity suggests that the universe as we know it is not an expression of God's intentions. It is a fallen cosmos, filled with creatures who have strayed from the way God wants them to follow. This, of course, raises a question: if God created the cosmos, why did he do so in a way that would result in our ignorance and disobedience to his will?

Traditional Christianity answers that God loves us, and out of that love gave us free will, but we have abused our freedom and have willed evil instead of good, resulting in our state of suffering and separation from God. It then teaches us that through acceptance of the salvation offered by Jesus in dying on the cross to cleanse us of our sins, we are reunited with God. After receiving our salvation, our task is to discern God's will and follow it.

This is not a very satisfying answer to the question of what is God's will and why there is evil in the universe. It blames the human race for freely choosing to contradict the will of God in the Garden of Eden, thus bringing suffering upon all generations since. But suffering is a lot older than our race. Outrageous brutality didn't begin with the free choice of human beings: consider the dinosaurs. If we look light-years backward in time, by looking at the most distant cosmic structures, we see suns vaporizing and galaxies colliding. It is a messy universe! The story of the Garden of Eden does not exonerate God from responsibility for all the horrors of the universe around us. The cosmos is full of evidence that the will of God includes all sorts of destruction and suffering.

At the same time, the observable cosmos around us also offers another view of the will of God. The evolution of life on earth appears to tend toward higher forms of consciousness over time. Human beings are far from being perfectly kind, loving, cooperative creatures. But our species has a capacity for goodness that is unparalleled by any other form of life in the natural history of the planet.

While it may take two steps forward, then three steps back, then five steps forward, then one step back, the cosmos does seem to develop in a certain general direction. There is pressure acting from within it to develop higher levels of complexity and consciousness. This development can also be described as an expression of the will of God. Insofar as we are graced with the ability to act in a manner that promotes higher consciousness, we are participating in the creation of the future to which the will of God seems aimed. Pursuing peace and justice, and practicing unconditional love even toward our enemies, hastens this future toward which our universe appears to be moving.

We have choices. Our bad choices aim us backward, toward the days of the dinosaurs. Our good choices aim us toward a future when love will create a world more wonderful than we can imagine. While the will of God can be said to have brought us into our current predicaments, the will of God also nudges us toward a future of love, peace, and justice. We have to exercise our free choice about this manifestation of divine purpose: will we cooperate and speed it up, or fight and slow it down?

◇

Discerning the will of God, and cooperating with it, is often a challenging and inexact affair. Life presents us with harsh choices.

Take the question of abortion. Banning it would violate the natural right of women to control their reproduction. Yet the choice to have an abortion is never a positive thing, no matter how many compelling reasons there are for making that choice. It seems that neither outlawing it nor allowing it will bring us any closer to the future that God wills for us. It stretches credulity to claim that God's will either sanctions or prohibits abortion.

Likewise, it isn't clear at all which economic system is congruent with the will of God. The Bible generally heaps condemnation on the quasi-capitalistic system practiced in the largely agrarian societies of ancient times. But the current industrial market economy dominating the planet presents us with a contradiction. It has created a truly global culture, broken down racial and national boundaries, and enabled many common people to live in comforts that were unimaginable in Jesus' time. This would appear to be consistent with God's will. But this system has also devastated the planet's natural environment and brutalized the lives of hundreds of millions of poor people. It would be presumptuous to declare that global capitalism, as opposed to any other social system, is the ultimate will of God.

My faith in the essential goodness of existence leads me to the hunch that the will of God—the unfolding plan of the universe—presses for peace, justice, and closer communion among people. But it isn't obvious how we ought to get there. Continually asking for the guidance of God, we learn from our mistakes. I question those who claim to know the fine print about God's will. As one of my seminary professors sagely remarked, the Ten Commandments provide many degrees of freedom: it's a short list consisting mostly of "don'ts." It's not a long list of what God *does* want us to do, which would make us slaves to a set of detailed rules. With only a few general prohibitions, agreed upon by almost everyone on the planet, we are given a lot of latitude to work out our response to the will of God for ourselves. And there's probably no way to do it except through intuition, trial, and error.

As I look back at that heartbreaking moment in the quiet room in the children's hospital, holding the lifeless body of that baby, I do find a hint about the will of God. The grief suffered by that child's parents was a dramatic expression of their love for him, a love that had seen beyond his deformities, beyond his limitations and sufferings. Likewise, the loving will of God aims beyond the sufferings and imperfections of the world around us—toward a new creation that will be "set free from its bondage to decay and will obtain the freedom of the glory of the children of God." (Romans 8:21)

14

Original Grace: The Road Beyond Sin

Amazing grace! How sweet the sound
That saved a wretch like me
I once was lost, but now am found
Was blind, but now I see. . . .

The doctrine of Jesus' substitutionary sacrifice on the cross to atone for the sins of humanity is central to traditional Christian belief. The doctrine says that humanity became hopelessly mired in original sin through the disobedience of Adam and Eve. Jewish law offered a way for Jews to achieve reconciliation with God, but it was impossible for anyone to fulfill its requirements completely. There was no way that humans could atone for their sins, either through their own efforts or through the practice of ritual sacrifice. So God sent his own son Jesus, who was sinless, to bear the sins of the world. Jesus' willing self-sacrifice on the cross satisfied God and erased the debt of sin of the whole human race. By accepting Jesus Christ, we are lifted of our burden of guilt against God for our sins.

It's an idea whose time has come—and gone.

The culture of the first century was one in which the ritual sacrifice of animals to God, or to the gods, was an everyday phenomenon. It was assumed that the gods were jealous, vengeful, and potentially capricious beings that had to be kept happy with the blood of the innocent and the aroma of cooked meat. It was also understood that blood was the very essence of life, and that it had a life of its own. Blood that was wrongfully shed demanded to be replaced through sacrifice.

When the metaphor of Jesus' crucifixion as substitutionary sacrifice was introduced, people understood the idea immediately. If we tried to practice blood sacrifice today, we would be arrested for violation of the laws preventing cruelty to animals. We live in a very different culture, in which ritual animal sacrifice is an abomination. We are utterly lacking a basis in everyday reality for the idea of blood sacrifice making penance for sin. I doubt that anyone would lobby for us to return to the cultural milieu in which such sacrifice once made sense. For this reason alone, the traditional doctrine of sacrifice/atonement, developed in the vastly different world people lived in 2,000 years ago, belongs in the boneyard of history.

Substitutionary sacrifice may be a relic of ancient culture, but amazing grace still abounds. It remains true that while we have the capacity to know and love God, we also inevitably suffer from sin. The biblical Greek word for sin, *amartia*, referred not only to individual evil acts, but also to a broader existential condition. It's not just the sinful act alone that's evil, but also its consequences: alienation from others, and from God.

In Jesus' time, people with certain diseases, occupations, and ethnicities were "sinful," alienated from the rest of the community because of their status, not because of any particular offense. Jesus had a special place in his heart for these "identified sinners," believing they had become scapegoats for the self-righteous ruling class. In word and actions, he extended grace to them.

Early Christianity had the insight that everyone suffers from this alienation. It is "original sin" in the sense that, as sentient beings, made in the image of God, we yearn for God because we feel a distance from our divine source. Because our distinct personalities create artificial boundaries between us, we long for reunion with the One from which we came. We inevitably suffer the consequences of our own bad choices and those of the cosmos around us. We suffer because we identify ourselves with our mortal nature. We suffer from the existential state of sin simply because we are human beings, not because we are especially wicked. But the grace of God redeems us from this existential condition, and restores us to our immortal nature. This is the good news of the gospel.

I experience this amazing grace in silent prayer. When in the quietude I pay attention to my thoughts, memories, urges, feelings, and relationships with others and with the world around me, I find myself drawn into greater and greater honesty. My resistance to seeing myself, warts and all, begins to break down. I begin to recognize and accept my reality, which is very far from perfect. Only then can I begin to change reality for the better.

In the moment that I most fully accept the truth of my failings, I simultaneously experience a great sense of relief. At this point, the Self that is God showers love on my ego self—my imperfect, mortal personality. And that forgiving love gives me the strength to move on, with a strong desire to seek a better way. This process is what traditional Christianity calls "confession" and "assurance of pardon."

But I do not need to beg pardon because I'm a hopeless sinner deserving eternal punishment for my evil acts. Human beings make choices that are sometimes good and sometimes destructive. Our existentially sinful condition does not imply that we are fundamentally bad beings. In fact, we are fundamentally good creatures; despite all our flaws, our ultimate purpose is to carry out our Creator's will, spreading God's love as widely as we can. We are good not because our past choices have been so wonderful, but because our existence has a mission of goodness. We are good because we are in the process of being formed in the image of a good God.

Traditional belief in the sinful nature of humanity results in the strange spectacle of good, morally upright, caring citizens getting down on their hands and knees and groveling about their hopelessly wicked state. Of course, every human being shares in the human condition of failure, suffering, and wrongdoing. But do we deserve to burn in hell for eternity, or to condemn ourselves as evil in this life, because of our God-given human condition? I don't think so.

Traditional Christianity says that God is good and made a good creation that includes human beings. Then it goes on to suggest that somehow human beings became bad, and the only way to make them good again was to pick one of them out and torture him to death so that the good God wouldn't have to torture all of them for eternity. This is a strange and unsatisfying argument.

The fact is that we already spend part of our time in hell, as a consequence of our existential condition and our failings. But we are more than failures. The universe is unfolding through us to reach higher and higher levels of consciousness. The real "at-one-ment" is not about substitutionary blood sacrifice. The real at-one-ment is about grace, which is our sense that life is a gift from God that has an intrinsic meaning and direction. My experience of God is grace-full. When I meditate, and become "at-one" with God, it feels like a gift. It isn't something I did as an ego or as a personality. It isn't "self-help." It is God-help, raising me up out of the consequences of my human condition and my mistakes to reach for a higher possibility and a larger purpose.

This is how I understand St. Paul's famous dictum that we are saved by grace and not by works (Ephesians 2:8-9). Paul described the grace of God as his saving action through Jesus' sacrificial death on the cross. That made sense in his day. What makes sense in our day is to recognize and admit that we can't escape our existential condition through self-help. We must open ourselves to the grace-filled presence of God.

The sacrifice we need today is not the slaughtering of birds, sheep, bulls, or human beings, as it was in ancient times. The sacrifice we need today is giving up our egos. We need to sacrifice our attachment to our identities, which will always be bound by our imperfections. No matter how hard we try to improve ourselves, no matter how hard we try to deny our failings, we will never be satisfied. We need to sacrifice our grasping for perfection, which will always be beyond our reach. No matter how often we work out in the gym, no matter how many years of college we attend, no matter how much psychotherapy we get, we will still be flawed beings. Instead, we need to open ourselves and receive the grace that is God within us. We need to discover that our true identity is "at-one" with God.

No longer must the cross represent the idea of substitutionary sacrifice. Instead, the cross can remind us of our existential condition: nailed by our failings, crucified by our grasp for perfection, dying of spiritual thirst from mad efforts to escape our weaknesses. And the cross can also remind us that, ultimately, we are not our bodies, we are not our egos, we are not our personalities.

The cross tells us we will always suffer, but we will always have access to saving grace. It is the crossroad at which we turn from our mortal selves—and grace-fully move toward our divine Selves.

15

Another Way
to Face the Cross

*He lay in the hospital bed, physically and emotionally devastated.
He was an older man, a member of College Heights Church. He had
just survived open-heart surgery and was recuperating. But the fear
he had suffered before the surgery, and the depression and
discomfort that followed it, were almost more than he could bear.
Then he remembered what would give him the strength to face
this ordeal.*

*He asked a nurse to take thumbtacks and form a cross on the
bulletin board facing his bed on the opposite wall. Then he fixed
his gaze on it and found comfort. While monitors beeped, and
nurses and doctors whisked around, the thumbtack cross gave him
solace. "It saved me," he told me, years after the experience.*

Imagine the enormous significance of the cross in the first centuries of the church, when it was still being used to kill anyone
who even appeared to challenge the authority of the empire! It
is a great marvel that the early Christians transformed this

Roman instrument of fear and death into a symbol with virtually the opposite meaning. The Christian cross is a homeo-
pathic remedy effective against the very function and purpose
of the Roman cross.

The early Christians found a model in the Old Testament
for the transformation of the cross into a symbol of spiritual
healing. The Old Testament myth tells us that God ordered
Moses to lift up a bronze serpent on a pole and show it to the
people; by gazing at this symbol of the source of their suffering
from snakebites, they were healed (Numbers 21:4-9). The New
Testament writers creatively extended this image by compar-
ing it to the cross of Christ. The Christ was lifted up on a cross,
so that we can also experience the life that transcends death
(John 3:12-17, 1 Peter 2:21-24).

A stick entwined with snakes is the symbol of medicine; it
became part of the Greek myth of the first doctor, Asklepius.
Who knows if the Old Testament and the Greek stories were
part of the same mythical legacy? In any case, the two myths
complement one another. The snake lives inside the earth, and
knows its secrets. It lives in the underworld of unconscious-
ness. By lifting it up, the secrets of the unconscious are
revealed, the causes of disease in life are exposed, and the hid-
den cures for disease are revealed as well.

The legend of Moses and the snake on the pole is an example of homeopathy: a dose of what ails us is the cure. The soul
also heals homeopathically. It isn't until we bring our spiritual
wounds to consciousness that we can begin to recover our
health and wholeness. Gazing at the cross stimulates the divine
life force within us. When we look at the cross, we see the truth
in Buddha's teaching that all life is suffering. This insight was
the beginning of Buddha's path to enlightenment. Likewise,
when we are fully able to face the suffering of the cross, we can
begin our own path to salvation.

In a time when we try to depersonalize suffering, denying
it or making it a fantasy for movies and television, the cross can
be a powerful force for healing. Jesus suffered, the people

around me suffer, I suffer. We cause each other harm, just as others caused Jesus harm. This is our truth. And in confessing this truth, a wound is opened in our soul through which God can enter. In gazing at the cross, our egos are crucified, and our divine nature is activated and made conscious. It is no longer I, the personality, contemplating the cross. It is God who gazes at it through me, and sees my ego and personality, as well as all others who suffer, nailed against it. God gazes with love that has healing power, love that resurrects us into new life.

The cross can take the form of any image that embodies or evokes the experience of suffering and mortality. Panhandlers on the streets are crucifixes for me. Having known so many of them personally, I am aware of the misery and heartache that led them to that life. I am confronted with their human condition of suffering, and my own mortality, when I am able to look them in the eyes as I encounter them on the sidewalks. If I give money, or not, the pain is still there—theirs and mine. Money won't make it go away, nor will words of stern advice, nor words of encouragement.

Panhandlers embody an important truth. If I can gaze at them with God's eyes of love, facing that truth and suffering it, not flinching from its existential discomfort, transcendence becomes possible. It is a chance to meet God face to face, to know the salvation that flows from the love that is God. And it is a moment to recommit myself to do what I can to alleviate that suffering, through direct personal action and by working for political and social change.

Anything in which we put false hope for salvation becomes a cross upon which we are crucified. We think computer technology will make life easy for us, then find ourselves nailed to keyboards night and day. We count on more money to bring us the happiness and security we've always craved, then find we've sacrificed our health and our families at the altar of the dollar. We put our hope for salvation from mortality into plastic surgeons, special diets, and exercise programs, only to discover we're immured by programs and products that torture us in the process of making us look more attractive.

By no means am I saying that technology is bad. (I wrote this book on a computer, set up a Web site to make a preliminary draft available for reading, and use e-mail as one of my primary communication tools.) Nor am I saying that hard work, professional fulfillment, vigorous exercise, and financial security are bad. They're very good—as long as they're kept, with everything else, in the right perspective; as long as they don't become false hopes and false gods with malevolent and inappropriate lives of their own.

Gazing at the cross can help us confront the false hopes and broken promises that can overwhelm us. It can jolt us back to the presence of the true God. It can serve as a much-needed tonic for the spirit, reminding us that while there is no escape from the human condition, the divine condition that Jesus showed us is there as well, available—and inviting. It holds out its arms for us.

PART V

Open Christian
Spiritual Practice

Now the
Greenblade
RISES

EASTER·1997· copy freely

16

Another Road
to Conversion

His conversion happened as a result of opening a jar of mayonnaise. It was the last item of food left in his house, all he had to feed himself and his young son. When he opened the jar and looked inside, he saw Jesus, inviting him to a totally different kind of life from the one he was living, in which moral dissipation had led to absolute poverty. His meeting with Jesus in the mayonnaise jar led him to accept the entire package of fundamentalist Christianity, immediately and unequivocally. When I met him, it was quite evident that this had been an enormously positive change. He was putting food other than mayonnaise on the table for his son, he had a job and was going to school, his attitude was positive, his demeanor was friendly and joyful. His was an abrupt, powerful, and quite genuine conversion.

She had a good job, a nice family, a comfortable home, but was deeply uneasy about her life. Something important was missing. She came to the Urban Ministry to volunteer. At our drop-in center for homeless people, she discovered divine compassion. She discovered the dimension that exists beyond success and achievement in one's career, beyond the surface contentment of a secure, upper-income lifestyle. She discovered God by spending one morning a week with people living on the streets. Her conversion was not traditionally Christian, although it led to her taking a great interest in Christianity. She didn't join a church, she didn't subscribe to a religious dogma. But she did become part of an informal community of people who shared her quest for spiritual deepening.

◇

His wife left him for another man, turning my friend's life upside down. He had seemed happy-go-lucky before this disaster struck. But after his wife left him, he saw how shallow his life had been. The only person with whom he had shared any intimacy was his wife, and now that she was gone, he saw that their relationship had been based on unspoken lies. He had avoided his inner life. He barely knew himself, and he didn't think he was worth knowing. He was emotionally shattered, angry at his ex-wife and himself. But then he started going to Co-Dependents Anonymous. He discovered spirituality through their 12-step program. He reached his soul, his own true nature. He didn't get his old life back—he got a better one. He felt for the first time as if his life were really his, a precious gift given to him by God, to live completely through thick and thin. His conversion was a decisive choice for a deeper kind of existence.

These latter two conversions were not the traditional Christian kind. They weren't about accepting Jesus as personal Lord and Savior. Yet all three conversion stories bear a strong resemblance to what happened to Jesus when he was baptized by John in the Jordan River, then immediately went into the desert to meditate for 40 days. There Jesus discovered his own deeper nature, the divinity within him. He "converted" to a much greater understanding of himself and the world around him. Afterwards, he was never the same. He left home and took to the road to become a wandering teacher and healer.

Conversion is a strong, fresh, spiritual experience that results in a significant shift in attitudes and actions. It can happen at many points in a person's lifetime. It is about much more than a decision to subscribe to a particular belief system.

"When did you accept the Lord?" is a common question among traditional Christians. My answer is that I had my first fully conscious encounter with the love that is God when I was 16 years old, during that backpacking trip in the Sierra Nevada. Throughout my childhood, I had felt that the world was enchanted with a wondrous quality and power beyond me; but that mountaintop moment of divine awareness was a pivotal point in my life. It was the beginning of my intentional spiritual practice.

Some of the most dramatic moments in life are religious conversions, when people turn away from one kind of life and faithfully embrace a better one. The history of the church is largely the long record of people who, over the centuries, have made decisive and sometimes dangerous decisions to become Christians. Conversion is and should be a cherished centerpiece of the religion; it has been the occasion for the spiritual and moral ennoblement of countless human beings.

Historically, there have been two ways in which people have become Christians. The first was conversion: the decision of an individual to take on a new religious identity. The New Testament chronicles dozens of such conversions to the early church.

The second means of becoming Christian is also described in the Bible. The head of a household would convert to Christianity and would bring all the members of his household—spouse, children, relatives, slaves—into the church with him, regardless of their own wishes. By the time the church became "Christendom"—the official, universal religion of Europe—this second means of becoming Christian was the norm. Baptism and confirmation sealed one's status as a Christian, but were not really understood as conversions. Almost all Christians, from the Middle Ages until a few hundred years ago, were born into the faith or forced into it by conquest. If you were not born into the church, you usually entered it because your king or chief had been baptized. And often your ruler did so for pragmatic reasons, such as saving his own life.

But throughout church history, and increasingly with the advent of Protestantism, there were those who held to the idea that the true church consisted of people who voluntarily, freely, and consciously chose to be Christians. They believed conversion was necessary even for those who had been born into the faith or had been grafted into it by circumstance. This position resonated strongly with the idea of individual freedom in a democracy of equals who form the institutions of society by voluntary association. It is no surprise that belief in the necessity of personal conversion, even for people born into Christian households, became a very powerful idea in American Christianity.

While the Christian church today is very much alive, Christendom is in a shambles. Christianity is no longer the official religion of Western civilization, which has largely separated church from state and religion from public life. Now, being a Christian is even more of a personal choice for individuals than ever. The phrase "I take Jesus Christ as my personal Lord and Savior" is a creedal statement of conversion devised by fundamentalist and evangelical American Christians. And the emphasis is on "personal." Traditional Christianity emphasizes that this is an individual decision, a free choice among other choices, not essentially different for a person raised in the church than it is for a person without a Christian background. Conversion may come as the result of a dramatic epiphany, a sudden circumstantial revelation of the truth of the faith. Or it may result from a slower process of spiritual discernment, a deliberate examination of one's own conscience.

But profound, genuine conversions happen outside the fundamentalist or evangelical conception of the experience. Conversion deserves a broader definition. It isn't necessarily about choosing to believe in a particular doctrine, or choosing somebody as your personal Lord and Savior. Conversion happens when people awaken to the divinity within themselves, and consciously choose to live in a manner consistent with this discovery. Conversion happens in as many ways as there are individual people who experience it.

The traditional Christian ritual of conversion is adult baptism. In some churches, only adults *can* be baptized. The ritual is performed when a person reaches puberty or is otherwise ready to make a conscious personal commitment to the Christian faith. Other churches baptize infants from Christian families. In these churches, the ritual can also be performed for adults who convert and wish to join the church, and repeated for adults who were baptized as children but want to reaffirm their vows as intentional adults.

It is my practice to baptize people as often as they wish. When John the Baptist performed the ritual at the Jordan River, it appears that individuals came to him repeatedly for baptism as a sign of their wish for repentance. I believe baptism is appropriate whenever a person reaches a decisive turning point and chooses the way of the spirit. It signifies a washing away of identification with the old self, and an infusion of the spirit that is God.

For Jesus, and for the rest of us, conversion is not so much about becoming a Christian as it is about the soul's discovery of God. Conversion is not just about turning to Jesus: it is about entering into the experience Jesus had when he found God within himself—the Christ.

17

Coming Home to Spiritually Centered Community

The moderator of the church welcomed me and ushered me inside the house to meet the rest of the committee seeking a minister for College Heights Church. I had never met any of these people before, but from the moment I sat down in their circle, I felt as if I had always known them.

It had been about eight years since I had worked as a parish minister, and I was not so sure about re-entering that role. I longed for a special kind of community where I could give and receive spiritual support. But I was afraid I would be burdened with all the accumulated baggage of church tradition I had successfully unloaded during my years of social service ministry.

However, my trepidation evaporated instantly upon entering that living room. I was joining them, not THE CHURCH as an amorphous, abstract entity. They were, and still are, a warm and wonderful extended family of real people with unique gifts and all the typical human failings. There was magic, a spiritual chemistry, that bonded us together from the beginning. I had come home.

I invite you to be joined by the church. Not a "Church Universal," but rather a particular, idiosyncratic, local manifestation of it. I say "be joined by" because that is usually the way we get connected to such communities. We find ourselves walking down the same road with a certain group of people, and eventually we discover that we belong with them.

This is what happened to Jim Corbett, a Quaker cattle rancher who lives in the desert outside Tucson. During the civil wars in Central America in the 1980s, he became involved in the effort to provide asylum for refugees who were streaming across the U.S.-Mexico border. Next thing he knew, he was part of a team of people—Quakers, Catholics, Presbyterians, and others with different or no religious backgrounds at all—challenging the policies of the Immigration and Naturalization Service by bringing refugees across the border in the Sonoran desert. The church had joined him through this particular band of people who had come together in faithful obedience and civil disobedience. He discovered that the church is very real even when it does not take the form of buildings with steeples or organizations with fixed doctrines.

"For where two or three are gathered in my name, I am there among them," said Jesus (Matthew 18:20). His name is love, and when even only a few people come together in this name, the church appears . . .

- ◆ *in small, informal groups that practice silent meditation.*
  I have participated regularly in such groups over the past 20 years. Outside of my family life, which is the ultimate test of spiritually centered community, these meditation circles have been the most significant form of the church for me.

- ◆ *in "12-step" groups such as Alcoholics Anonymous or Co-Dependents Anonymous.* These groups, which are centered on experiencing God without a complex theology, are among the most vital expression of the church today.

They practice a straightforward but very challenging spirituality that has evolved beyond traditional Christianity in some respects.

◆ *in men's and women's support groups, Bible or book study groups, drumming circles, yoga and tai chi classes, and any other small group that acknowledges and supports spiritual experience.* I have witnessed the transformative power of such groups, particularly those that are open-minded and open-hearted, guided by consensus, and led by lay people. One of the most important roles for the institutional church is to create, promote, and support such groups.

◆ *in Taizé worship.* Taizé services are proliferating around the world, giving Christians a beautiful new way to *be* the church. Taizé is an ecumenical Christian community in France that created a simple, meditative, moving candlelight worship service of chants, readings from the Bible, and veneration of the cross. It is an especially fertile meeting ground for people of Protestant and Catholic backgrounds. People don't "join" Taizé: it is more of a movement than a formal organization. Taizé demonstrates that a simpler form of the church can keep alive the best of the rich symbols, language, and rituals of the faith.

◆ *in service or social change efforts that are rooted in spirituality.* For several years I was director of such a group. The Urban Ministry was sponsored by a wide range of local churches and synagogues, and as such we did not profess a particular religion. But because we made it clear that spirituality was the wellspring of our actions, many volunteers and clients came to us for the same reasons people join traditional churches. Our organization created a place where people could explore and live out their faith, with the active support of a community of others who wanted the same thing.

- *in the workshop and event circuit.* Increasingly, people find spiritual community by attending weekend retreats and going to hear speakers at special events. Attending short-term workshops and speaker events is an excellent alternative to the old-fashioned church system in which one preacher does the talking, week after week, to the same group of folks.

  However, I have noticed that after a while people who become involved in the workshop circuit become homesick for a steady group of people with whom they can develop spiritual intimacy on a regular basis. There is synergy in doing both: as a minister in a church, I am delighted when our members get educated and energized at conferences and workshops, then come back to our congregation and share what they have discovered.

- *in congregations.* Local churches are vital building blocks of society. They enable individuals to be of service to their wider communities. And they nurture the bodies and souls of people throughout the cycles of life. Churches usually include people of all "ages and stages," giving each other spiritual support through their shared birth-through-death journeys, and mutually validating the meaning and purpose of life.

  Today the denominational affiliation of a church is less a guide than it used to be in choosing a congregation that fits a particular individual. Each local church is unique. The United Church of Christ congregation I serve as minister is quite content to be a small congregation of free-spirited people who practice meditation, engage in community service, and explore Christian and other spiritual traditions. At the other extreme, there are very large churches featuring great diversity, and offering literally dozens of small group experiences in addition to huge worship services.

In my opinion, the churches that offer their members the best opportunity for true spiritual fulfillment—regardless of denomination—are those that have an open-minded, minimalist approach to creeds and doctrines; respect the individual conscience in matters of faith and practice; and focus most on experiencing God and least on the personality or charisma of a particular leader.

As the above discussion implies, traditional church organization is one way to express Open Christian community, but not the only way. The church is undergoing a rapid transformation away from hierarchical denominational structures. There is a proliferation of alternative ways for people to support each other in the life of faith. The church exists to create the kingdom of heaven on earth, and that kingdom will contain many manifestations of spiritually centered community life.

The last book of the Bible, the Revelation to John, ends with a glorious mythical vision of the world to come (Revelation 21). It is a vision of a magnificent city that descends from heaven, with 12 open gates into which people stream from every nation. One of the most striking aspects of this vision is that, unlike the old Jerusalem, the New Jerusalem does not have a temple. The entire city is holy, dedicated to the glory of God. God and the Lamb—the Christ—are enthroned in the city, but they are not described as having human form, and there are no churchy trappings around them.

We can find hints of this vision in the religious history of America. Lancaster County, Pennsylvania, center of the Amish culture, is a valley of gorgeous farms and beautiful people living in unusual harmony with each other and with the land. The Amish are very traditional Christian people, so an outsider would expect to find Amish church buildings dotting the landscape, but there aren't any to be seen. The Amish don't build them. They believe that *they are* the church. Their farms are their sanctuaries; they meet for worship in each others' living rooms.

Another version of the vision is embodied in the small towns of New England. The New England town *was* a church congregation. The New England Congregational church building had two functions: a place of worship, and seat of the town's governance through direct democracy. The plainness of the church building expressed the idea that the church was not an entity separate from the town itself. The church was not to be found in the building, but among the people, whose everyday life was supposed to have a spiritual focus.

The institutional Christian church aims at something better than itself. Its purpose is to help transform human society into a multiracial, multicultural community of peace, justice, harmony, beauty, and reverence. Should we ever realize this vision, there may be no need for separate church buildings, clergy, or complicated religious hierarchies.

All too often, churches lose sight of this goal and become preoccupied with their own propagation and self-preservation. The Church sometimes clings to its rituals and jargon as ways of maintaining a superior and separate identity. But in the New Jerusalem, religious or cultural affiliation will become secondary. Revelation says of the holy city, "People will bring into it the glory and the honor of the nations." (21:26)   As I read this vision, the various cultures of the world and their religious traditions aren't to be wiped out and replaced with "Christian dominion." Instead, people of all cultures and religions are gathered together to share their common delight in the presence of God. It is a vision of the fulfillment of the Church's mission in the world.

Local churches are ideally situated to respond to a wide range of basic human needs, ranging from spiritual growth groups, to programs that feed the hungry, to efforts to reform the social and political order. The local congregation is a basic unit of American society, giving people in this vast and lonesome land a sense of belonging. The local church is often the only viable alternative for providing a vibrant community life, because the roles of the extended family and the neighborhood have largely collapsed in this country.

My work as a church minister has frequently involved organizing support groups and service programs that spin off to become independent of our church organization. Around the world, a staggering number of service groups and institutions have been started by churches. This legacy follows from Jesus' compassionate actions, as well as from the practical reality that churches are grass-roots communities poised to act as local organizers. Each of these churches has a special stone to lay in the foundation of the New Jerusalem.

I have often observed that the most important time at church is coffee hour. It seems that worship is just a prelude, a way to get ready for this time when kids frolic in the social hall and adults check in with each other while sipping from steaming cups. Coffee hour offers a place where folks will ask about you if you don't show up.

At its best, the church is a community where all kinds of people can honor each other for who they really are—many sparks from the one divine fire, each with a true Self that is one with God. In a sterile landscape of shopping malls and industrial parks, amid a culture that glorifies mayhem and murder in its blockbuster movies, in a world in which intimate human relationships are trivialized, the church inspires delight in the "vertical dimension" of life. The church in all its forms can make our human experience divine through worship, contemplation, and loving service. Alongside the communities of other faiths, local Christian churches have much to contribute to the creation of the heavenly city on earth.

18

A Walk with God

I could hardly wait for God to take me for a walk. Like a restless dog waiting for his mistress to come home from work, I was full of wild and eager energy. My mind raced with schemes and dreams, unresolved conflicts and unrealistic ambitions, jumbled together and bouncing off my body's walls like puppies bumping into furniture.

Finally it was time to leave the office, head for home, and stop for my walk along the way. Fumbling with my keys, I got into the car, moving faster than I needed to move. I drove toward the trailhead, stuck in traffic as usual, wanting the lights to change before their time, silently cursing the drivers ahead of me as if their careless moves were personal insults. My mind continued its excited-dog behavior, running in circles, spinning and panting.

At the park, I bounded out of the car, locked and slammed the door. God struggled to keep me on the leash, to get hold of my mind and body and synchronize me with her intentions. Like a dog choking himself on his collar while straining to sniff every tree and bush, I strained against the leash of my own physical and mental limitations. I wanted to get away, be free, escape the daily grind. But I was held by powers greater than myself.

My walk was not about escaping myself and the everyday world I allowed to drive me stir-crazy. It was about adjusting to the tension against my leash, keeping pace with God as she walked behind me, a close presence. After a while, I relaxed into a more natural cadence, keeping rhythm with my Mistress. A mile down the trail, enjoying the sunlight through the fog and the rustling of the stiff live oak leaves in the breeze, I realized that the pace my Mistress keeps is in fact the same pace that is most natural for me. I walked ahead of my Mistress, yet I subtly perceived her guiding hand, directing me in my walk without hearing her commands or feeling the force of her arm. Somehow, she let me know where we were going together. Our walk became a joy, a quiet celebration of our companionship on the trail.

By the time I got back to the car, I was in a vastly different state of mind and body. Gently, my Mistress let me back in the car. Calmly, I took my place behind the wheel and drove home. Another day, another walk with God.

It's natural to experience God. It is grace, a gift, that each of us was born to receive. There is a God-shaped place in every human being, ready to receive the Dear One in the heart and soul. It is a blessing bestowed on us from beyond. But we won't experience that blessing fully if we just remain passive in its presence. We need to exercise our souls.

It's easy to forget that we are spiritual beings. It's easy to ignore that our souls hunger and thirst for spiritual bread and wine. It's easy for us to confuse our deepest needs and desires with our less vital urges. We find ourselves ruminating compulsively about our physical and social needs, confusing the urge for these things with the deeper desire to be one with God and the universe. Just as it is natural to know God, it is unfortunately also quite natural to forget God.

The most I would claim for myself is that after years of spiritual practice, I now recognize that I'm out of touch with God fairly quickly after any incident that I allow to get in love's way. I'm a lot better at apologizing when I needlessly hurt other people's feelings. I'm better than I used to be at noticing when my mind and body are off-center, drifting into obsession about things that are negative or don't really matter.

Part of this change is due to the natural maturation process. We really do get a bit wiser as we get older. But I'm sure this change is also due to my intentional spiritual practice over the years. If I miss my two weekly meditation sessions, I notice the difference. I can detect a lack of serenity, a dulling of my sense of awe and wonder, in those times when I fail to keep my discipline. Likewise, I am amazed at how flat and dull my world becomes after an extended period when I don't keep my journal or do any writing. I begin to see the world only as it is packaged and presented by my calendar, the media, billboards, by the mass culture that surrounds me. My spiritual disciplines have trained me to *notice* when I've lost my way home to the divine heart of love and creativity.

I can't count the times I have sat down at the keyboard, knowing it will be good exercise for my soul to do some writing, but having no idea what I'm going to write about. One, maybe three hours later—I can't tell—I look back at what I have written in amazement; not so much at the quality of my work, but at the quantity and richness of its content. I often tell my wife that my head has no idea what I'm going to write, but my fingers know exactly what to say! The writing often comes from a place in my heart and soul of which I'm not conscious at all.

But the spiritual discipline of writing does require conscious volition. I'm not in a hypnotic state when I first sit down at the keyboard. The conscious discipline opens a channel into the unconscious that transcends the discipline itself. This is true of all spiritual exercise.

Paying attention to dreams has also been a helpful spiritual practice, and I have recorded many significant dreams in my journal. For a while, our church had a "dream group" that met weekly. Participants told their dreams and explored their meanings. We saw common themes and images among our dreams, reminding us how intimately connected we are at soul level.

The Bible includes many dreams. Some predicted future events. Other dreams gave deep insight and understanding to the people who had them, providing them with images they could use to make sense of their circumstances. Dreams are ways to experience God if we make a conscious effort to remember, record, and reflect upon them.

I take a long walk every day by myself, either in my neighborhood or in the local open-space preserves. This has become a very important spiritual as well as physical exercise for me. I love to walk in solitude, keeping a fast pace, opening my senses to the environment surrounding me. I attempt to be fully present, truly aware of the redwood trees and vistas, the flowers amidst the chaparral, even the very dirt upon which I tread.

I'm often amazed at how impervious my heart and soul can be to the astounding beauty all around me as I walk. Suddenly I'll realize I have covered two miles without really being aware of my surroundings along the trail. In those moments, I invoke divine compassion on my forgetfulness, then find myself straining to stay awake from the sleep that so often passes for normal wakefulness.

Those sudden awakenings on the trail are moments of grace. I did not summon them, I did not earn them. But the moments after them are chances for me to exercise spiritual discipline, to exercise my will to remain aware and awake to the presence of God all around me. Spiritual discipline is a response to grace. When you receive a precious present from someone you love, you are willing to work hard to protect, preserve, and appreciate it.

Keeping silence, walking, sojourning in wilderness—these are Christian disciplines. Jesus withdrew to the desert for 40 days at the beginning of his ministry, and he headed for the hills or the Garden of Gethsemane on many occasions to maintain his connection with God. He became disturbed and distracted by the world and the people around him—just as we do. He needed to break his routines intentionally so he could "re-member" himself in the presence of God.

It helps to have some form of spiritual discipline with a group, for the same reasons that we do physical disciplines on teams or in classes. This is another important Christian insight about the needs of the human soul. Jesus did not gather 12 disciples just to guarantee himself an audience; he needed a steady community around him to provide encouragement and to keep himself honest. We are social beings. We get validation and friendly criticism when we join together to invigorate our bodies and souls.

In my own practice, I find it helpful to have a group of people with whom I feel comfortable sharing some of the thoughts and feelings that arise in meditation. Difficult and disturbing experiences that I force out of my everyday awareness sometimes arise out of the silence. It feels safe to share these as well as the ecstatic, euphoric moments that occasionally arise in meditation with a group of fellow meditators who won't assume I'm crazy when I report them.

Spiritual practice can be difficult, because it requires conscious effort in the face of the countless distractions of everyday existence. And there's risk: it can open one up to painful memories or repressed feelings. But in spiritual practice we rediscover that God is readily available, offering compassion.

Worshipping in church is a communal discipline, a time set apart for centering ourselves in God. As Jesus said, "The sabbath was made for humankind, and not humankind for the sabbath." (Mark 2:27) Worship is a spiritual exercise we employ to overcome our natural forgetfulness of the divine presence.

I am convinced that the ancient Hebrew concept of the Sabbath, carried on by Christian weekly worship, is based on human beings' natural rhythm. As there is a natural rhythm of waking in the morning and sleeping at night, so is there a rhythm of being awake to the presence of God, then slowly drifting off into the "sleep" of the humdrum and the everyday. Again and again, I have heard the same phrase from church members: "Sunday worship recharges my spiritual batteries!"—batteries that seem to run no more than seven days without some kind of intentional re-energizing.

Just like physical exercise, spiritual discipline can be strenuous, but its ultimate purpose is to invigorate the soul. At times it is immensely pleasurable; at other times it is painful to break through to a deeper, more lasting connection with God. The great mystical teachers of Christian history reported periods of "spiritual dryness" or "dark nights of the soul" through which they exerted great fortitude in order to continue in their spiritual practices. Jesus' spiritual discipline was sometimes refreshing—his baptism in the River Jordan, for example. And sometimes it was painfully difficult, as his agony in the Garden of Gethsemane reminds us. There are times when the phrase "no pain, no gain" applies to the soul's quest for God as it applies to our physical bodies.

Being of service to others has been a powerful form of spiritual practice for me. My soul was exercised daily when I worked for nine years with people in extreme poverty. I found God in my relationships with them. People in crisis have an uncanny knack for making the rest of us question our assumptions.

Trying to love people our culture tells us are unlovely is a very effective way of getting us to confront our own fears about suffering and loss of dignity. More than anything else, homeless and otherwise marginalized people taught me that life is about loving each other through all the suffering that comes with the human condition. I used to think that suffering was an aberration, something that is not supposed to happen. But after years of staring it in the face every day on the streets, I am now convinced that suffering will be with us for a long time. Our task is to alleviate it wherever and however we can, stand with those in anguish, and celebrate those interludes when we enjoy health and happiness.

We live in a culture that depersonalizes pain, and attempts at every turn to deny it and drug it. It takes real discipline to face suffering at all, much less to commune deeply with people in crisis. This kind of compassionate service is integral to Christianity. It began with the mercy Jesus offered to the sick and troubled people he encountered along his road.

"Just a closer walk with thee
Grant it Jesus if you please
Daily walking close with thee
Let it be, dear Lord
Let it be . . ."

The words of that beloved old hymn are a prayer for divine intimacy. But we need to do more than just ask: it takes the active effort of spiritual discipline to stay on the road where we can meet and walk with God.

19

Coming Home to Worship

I was invited to preach at a black Baptist church. It was a congregation of about 75 members, and when I arrived it seemed that all of them were in attendance. This little church, crammed into its broken-down building, had four choirs—each of them excellent. I discovered that I was one of three preachers for the day. The service took about three hours. There was no need for a printed church bulletin, an item considered essential in churches like my own. In the midst of the wonderful singing, the intensity of call-and-response between preacher and congregation, someone in the pews spontaneously called out: "Mrs. Washington! Play your harmonica for us!" The rest of the congregation urged her on. With an "Aw, shucks," the old woman stood and pulled a harmonica out of her purse and started to play. It sounded awful—sour notes, a broken tune. I winced, both for her and for her audience.

But the congregation amen-ed and hallelujah-ed with just as much gusto as they had done for their wonderful choirs, solo singers, and preachers. I was moved to tears by this profound lesson: true worship is any sincere, heartfelt, best effort to adore God. It is what the wise men did when they "were overwhelmed with joy" in finding the newborn Christ. It is what we will all do in the heavenly city of the New Jerusalem.

I have kept the spiritually pregnant silence of a colonial Quaker meeting house in Maryland, sung the hauntingly beautiful chants of the Mass in a Catholic church in Minnesota, seen fresh glimmers of light come out of the Scripture during Bible study in a fundamentalist worship service in rural Colorado. I have sung Pentecostal hymns in Spanish in a squatters' community church in Mexico (the members of the congregation had constructed its walls out of flattened five-gallon tin cooking-oil cans, creating very unusual acoustics). I have witnessed the piety of pilgrims standing in long lines to light candles and kiss the icons in the Orthodox shrine of St. Sergius in Russia. I have worshipped sitting on the floor, my legs tucked behind me, as a Buddhist monk blessed the new year for a community of Laotian refugees in San Francisco. Every day at Stanford, I listen to the low wail of Muslim prayers coming from the meeting room of the Islamic Students Association across the hall from my office. I am convinced that the urge to worship is universal among human beings, and that there are many valid ways to satisfy it. At the same time, I can appreciate the reasons so many people don't feel comfortable in Christian worship.

Most Americans call themselves Christians, but only about 20 percent of them attend worship on any given Sunday. There can be only one reason for this: most of the worship services the churches offer are no longer meaningful for a very high percentage of people. They don't want to be "pew potatoes," passively sitting through a dull worship service merely out of habit or obligation. And of those who do attend worship, many are bored to distraction by the services, and come only because they love the people in their church communities and share the values that the church upholds.

I feel at home in the worship service of the church I serve as minister, but even so, I am sometimes bothered by the lyrics of old familiar hymns to which many of our members have sentimental attachments. Many people both inside and outside the church no longer find emotional or spiritual value in traditional worship. All too often, worship either requires a master's degree in theology to be understood, or is painful to intellectual and aesthetic sensibilities.

Many churches try to enliven worship with rock bands, song lyrics projected by big monitors on the sanctuary walls, and made-for-TV preaching. But such services still seem bizarre to people who have lost, or never had, any attachment to traditional Christian worship. Such upbeat, jazzy church services are symptoms of the problem, not solutions to it. They are sugar coatings on a pill that is still hard for most people to swallow.

To understand how this happened, we need to look back to the very beginnings of Christianity. Worship in the early Christian church wasn't a slick marketing tool for evangelism. Nor was it a mere ritual enactment to which its members had a sentimental attachment. Nor was it merely a divine requirement that had to be fulfilled. Rather, it was a meaningful expression of the current, shared experience of its members.

Later, as Christianity became the institutional religion of Western civilization, the Mass became a rite that had to be continued to keep body and soul together, both for individuals and for society. Even if nobody showed up, Mass would still have to be performed by the priest on behalf of the people. Mass became a sacrifice that the church was required to offer God, and in turn, God offered grace and salvation to the people through the church. The people did not worship, really: the church worshipped for them, then gave the people the wafer of bread that had been mystically transformed into the body of Christ, the means of their salvation. Worship was a sacred drama, modeling in religious ritual the relationship between subjects and sovereign both in its earthly and cosmic manifestations.

Protestant churches broke with this long tradition, rejecting the mystical nature of the Mass, declaring that the ceremony of the bread and the wine was only symbolic, and instead focusing worship on reading and interpreting the Bible. Salvation was available only through personal faith, and faith had to be grounded in Scripture. Before the Reformation, the saving grace of God came through the wafer that the church mystically transformed into the body of Christ. Post Reformation, saving grace came from a book called the Bible, which had been mystically transformed into the Word of God.

Today most people know that their salvation is dependent neither upon the church nor the Bible. Most people know they can experience the grace of God apart from organized religion. So the place of worship in Christianity has forever changed. Worship is no longer an obligation upon which one's place in immortality depends. And it is no longer something the church needs to do on our behalf to fulfill God's expectations. Thus liberated, worship can become the free expression of sincere gratitude and delight for the presence of God.

A new view of worship can benefit by starting with a look at the enduring qualities of traditional worship. For all its overtones of superstition, Eucharistic worship (the Mass of liturgical churches such as Catholics, Episcopalians, and Lutherans) can be very satisfying, if for no other reason than the sense of tradition and devotion that its rich aesthetic evokes. A first-time visitor to a highly liturgical worship service can pick up a sense of its mystery and spiritual appeal, without comprehending the content at all. Indeed, many Catholics wish that the Mass were still said only in Latin.

Sometimes we need to worship at a level deeper than the rational mind. The Mass is a powerful system of symbols, giving the worshipper a poetic language of images and words that can express the depths of spiritual experience. Protestant worship often seems graceless by comparison. It is no wonder that in recent years, many Protestant churches, sensing their historical overreaction to Catholicism, have added Eucharistic liturgical elements to their worship services.

The Reformed Protestant tradition, of which I am a product, centers worship on the sermon. To this day, preaching can be a high art and provide inspiration for deep communion of souls with God. It can synthesize the rational and the emotive aspects of faith. A good sermon can convince and comfort, bring tears and laughter, edify and motivate people to action, all in the space of 20 minutes. But in an age where there is so much access to high-quality communication, a mediocre sermon is worse than no sermon at all. People rightly ask themselves why they should bother listening to sermons that are not excellent. If they don't find good preaching in the church, they can find it on tape, or read the written equivalent in books or magazines, or surf for it on the Internet.

A fast-growing branch of Christianity today is the Pentecostal movement, which worships under the immediate influence of the Holy Spirit. Pentecostalism is ecstatic, improvisational, and emotionally engaging. Utterance coming from an altered state of consciousness—"speaking in tongues"—is the focus of worship. The authority of this experience is based on the day of Pentecost (Acts 2:1-13), when the disciples gathered after the death and resurrection of Jesus. They suddenly began to speak to a crowd using languages other than their own. This original "speaking in tongues" was not the apparent gibberish of modern-day Pentecostals, but rather real-world languages that visitors to Jerusalem from various lands around the Roman world could understand.

The original gift of tongues was the instantaneous ability to speak a language that you had never studied or understood before. This myth was a reversal of the tale of the tower of Babel (Genesis 11:1-9). Nervous about the construction of a tower that was reaching ominously close to heaven, God decided to stop the building project by confusing the workers with different languages. The proliferation of different languages in the world was considered a curse until the Pentecost moment. Through a new multicultural community called the church, it was turned into a blessing, a sign of a new covenant between God and humanity. The "babble" of Pentecostals who speak in tongues is an expression of spiritual ecstasy that is found in many traditions both within and outside of Christianity.

It is ironic that speaking in tongues is the opposite of what happened in the Book of Acts, where people heard the disciples speaking directly to them in their own real languages. But Pentecostal Christianity still shows us the possibility of a truly multicultural form of the faith. The most racially integrated worship services I have attended have been in Pentecostal churches. The movement holds out the promise that the Spirit can bring people together across the borders of ethnicity and language.

I am fascinated by the kinds of worship people do without even being consciously aware of it. Consider the millions of people who flock to rock concerts. Few of them would call this activity "worship," yet there is something highly formalized about it. There is devotion, coming from the experience of being a fan of the musician or group. The "clergy"—musicians—wear characteristic garb and appearances that are not appropriate in "secular" contexts (long or weird hair, body piercing, tattoos, distinctive clothing, etc.). There is liturgy: a list of songs for which the fans faithfully wait. There are congregational responses: cheering, clapping, singing, dancing, and sometimes ecstatic swooning. There are rituals: the mosh pit, rushing the stage, tossing promotional materials out to the crowd, an intermission, and a finale.

Consider graduation, that supreme worship ritual of our educational system. The "clergy"—professors and administrators who, 500 years ago, were indeed clergymen controlling the educational establishment—dress in medieval academic robes reminiscent of clerical vestments, and bestow "grace" upon the new graduates in the form of diplomas instead of wafers of bread. Likewise, the world of business is rife with ritual. Management seminars, motivational speakers, workshops: many of these feel a lot like religious events, and certainly a great deal of the content is reminiscent of what the Protestant Reformers rejected as hocus-pocus in the Catholic Mass.

People worship. They get together to celebrate values that transcend themselves as individuals. They get together to express their devotion to that transcendence. One way or another, consciously or unconsciously, we try to satisfy our innate need to worship.

I envision a day when worship becomes a much more public and overtly spiritual expression. I yearn for the day when there are no adversarial feelings between separate sects of "true believers," each thinking the others are worshipping false idols. I dream of a time when churches and temples and synagogues band together to produce public interfaith worship events that blend the best of their legacies with the best of current artistic and musical forms. I hope that more and more popular musicians and performers will overtly invoke the sacred dimension during their concerts and festivals, without doing so in a divisive, sectarian manner.

Perhaps these hopes will come to pass. Some churches are experimenting with different blends of ancient Christian ritual and current language, music, and visual media in worship, abandoning ritual elements that don't make sense anymore, and developing new ones that can speak for our souls today.

In my ministerial role, I have found it possible to create worship experiences that evoke the same sense of the holy that traditional ritual does, but without using traditional theology. The church I serve has about 80 members, of which 35 or so are typically in attendance at Sunday worship. Most of our members chose our church because it is a small, intimate group. People wear casual clothes and meet in a semicircle in front of our communion table. We sing chants—brief, repetitive pieces of music—in Latin, Greek, Spanish, English, and Sanskrit. Many of the chants we use are from the Taizé community in France. A Tibetan brass bowl is our prayer bell, calling us to a period of silence and a time to light candles as signs of our intentions in prayer. The lighting of candles by people in the congregation has become an especially potent moment in our worship. The readings are usually from the Bible, but sometimes we read modern poetry or prose, or writings from other religious traditions. After the sermon, there is always a time for discussion.

At the end of worship, we stand in a circle around the communion table. Once a month we share the bread and wine of the Eucharist, which in our church can be taken by anyone, whether baptized or not. We have time for brief sharing about our lives, then we say or sing the Lord's Prayer and sing another chant to end the service. Ours is a blend of the mystical, non-rational, artistic aspects and the intellectual, verbal, social aspects of worship.

Our service omits a number of traditional Christian worship elements. While we certainly make reference in prayers to our need for forgiveness and reconciliation with each other and with God, we don't use the traditional litanies of confession and absolution. We don't recite the Apostles' Creed, because few of us agree with all its declarations.

Our form of worship evolves continually. We have a monthly open meeting to review and plan it. The congregation is quite open to new and different forms of worship, and sometimes we deviate considerably from our typical liturgy. It is truly the worship expression of a particular, local, small group of people who form a close-knit community. I think we have developed some beautiful and creative worship services from which other churches might glean useful ideas. But I cannot imagine "canning" our service and exporting it whole into other congregations. What we do is idiosyncratic to our own needs and our unique mix of members.

But there is one principle that is fully exportable from College Heights United Church of Christ: worship is a creative exercise. It isn't just a given from the past to be carried on, unchanged forever, into the future. By our willingness to remove outmoded portions, reinterpret others, and add new elements as we are inspired, we are more able to give God wholehearted praise and glory.

20

Inward Mobility: Rites and Passages

It would have been a joyous occasion in any case. The parents, members of our church, were delighted at the birth of their healthy baby boy. We baptized him as we stood in a circle around our communion table. One of our members, a potter, had made a chalice with a butterfly motif inside the bowl. We passed it, filled with water, around the circle of family members and people of our congregation. One by one, they took the baptismal chalice, dipped their fingers in the water, and spoke blessings for the child. Then the bowl returned to me, and I dipped my fingers into the water and made the sign of the cross on the baby's forehead.

Everyone present held in their memory this baby's older brother, who had died in infancy due to severe birth defects. When they touched the water, some of the people blessed the memory of the dead child as they blessed the happy reality of the newborn. The joy at this baptism was made even more potent by our recognition of the precious fragility of life.

The baptism marked a wonderful beginning for the parents of the baby, and it also marked the end of the time of acute grief

about his brother's death. There was great joy heightened by sweet
sadness that filled the room as the chalice passed around the circle.

Rituals are mirrors. They help us see ourselves—not just the surface appearances, but the depths of our being. Rituals give us a language of words, stories, sights, and movements to help us connect our conscious and unconscious realms. They help us feel what we need to feel.

The baptism of the child helped us let out our feelings of gratitude and released us from a period of mourning. To reach our innermost places, thoughts aren't enough. Our actions in the visible, audible, tangible dimension give life and breath to our invisible, inaudible, intangible dimension. If the chemical substance of the water itself imparted the desired effect of the baptism, it would be more time- and energy-efficient for me to just pick up the bowl myself and forget about passing it around the circle. But the movement of the bowl from hand to hand mirrored the spiritual connection among the people in the circle. The inward experience of that outward act stimulated a communion among our souls. Because each person in the congregation touched the water, when I made the sign of the cross with the water on the child's forehead, I imparted the blessing of everyone present. These physical movements of our bodies evoke a corresponding spiritual movement in our souls.

The transitions of life can be very upsetting. The birth of a child is a joyous occasion, but it turns the world of the new parents upside down. Marriage is a happy thing, but it is also the occasion for major changes in family relationships that can be confusing and painful. It goes without saying that puberty and death cause tumult in family life. The meanings that life used to have are challenged by these transitions. People often feel guilty that they are sad after events they think should be happy, or feel guilty that they are relieved after events they think should be occasions for grief. Ritual helps people express this normal and natural mix of feelings and make sense out of life once again, integrating important events into the stories of their lives in deeply satisfying ways.

Birth, puberty, marriage, and death: these are the times people find they need ritual whether they think of themselves as religious or not. It isn't enough just to experience these life transitions ourselves or to watch them happen to others, and leave it at that. People sense that each life passage has meaning, but they often have trouble expressing it. They need a way to access the meaning.

Ritual can express this meaning at many levels—sensual, intellectual, poetic, emotional, spiritual. Sacred Christian rituals include the Eucharist (more commonly known as communion, or the Lord's Supper), baptism, confirmation, penance, anointing the sick, matrimony, and the ordination of clergy. The Christian tradition is an immense treasury of different ways to perform each of these sacraments. With creative and sensitive adaptation, they can continue to be powerful contributors to our spiritual practice as we evolve beyond Christian orthodoxy. For example, confirmation can migrate from being a time for teenagers to become official church members into being a ritual that celebrates the soul's transition from childhood to adulthood, a time when God incarnates in a new way in the young person's body and soul.

As another example, in our church the tradition of anointing the sick has been integrated into the worship service. People can come forward to the communion table during the time for silent prayer and receive the sign of the cross with oil on their foreheads as a sign of their intentions for healing, for themselves and others. By extending traditional rituals to apply to a wider range of people and experiences, they are more able to serve their purpose in giving meaning to the important passages of life.

Rituals give us *inward mobility*. The movements of the ceremony take us to places in our souls that would otherwise be hard to reach.

◈

When we met for the first time to begin planning their wedding, I asked the couple to tell me how they met and fell in love. She began her side of the story by talking about her life before she met him. "The period of darkness—that's what I call it!" she said. Not that she had been miserable and depressed. She had a good career, lots of friends and a warm family. But it all seemed dim compared to the light she experienced after she met him. In equally glowing terms, he described how she had brought him joy he never dreamed he could know. I could tell this was going to be an extraordinary wedding.

I always ask couples if they would like to write their own vows, but usually they prefer to choose from a collection of vows I give them to consider. Not so with this couple: they said they would write their own, and surprise each other with them during the wedding.

It was a simple service, outdoors in an enclosed garden in a city park on a lovely summer evening. The time came for the sharing of the vows. Her vow to him brought me to tears. When it was his turn, his best man gave him his guitar, and he sang his vow to her in the form of a song he had written. Then everyone's eyes were sparkling with tears.

My tears were those of joy for this beautiful couple. But they were also tears of grief, because my first marriage was coming to an end. In them, I was reminded how beautiful love can be, and in my own life I was watching how beautiful love can die. The wedding I was performing helped me feel the grief I needed to feel, even as it wonderfully expressed the meaning of the love between this bride and groom.

Rituals are screens against which we project our own feelings and interpretations. Having looked around the crowds at hundreds of weddings, and having seen the range of expressions on people's faces, I observe that there are as many meanings in a wedding as there are people in attendance. For some, it is a reminder of the joy or awkwardness of their own wedding days. For others, it brings up feelings of longing or frustration, wishing themselves at the altar in the place of the bride or groom. For yet others, it is an occasion for reflection on the joys and challenges of keeping their marriages together. For me, on the day of that particular wedding, it was an occasion to grieve the dying of the embers of my first marriage.

I tell couples to be prepared for these projections as the time of the wedding approaches, because they often result in strange behavior by otherwise nice people. Family and friends know the wedding will be a powerful event that will touch their hearts, so they often become nervous and awkward during preparations for the ceremony. Obsessing about details that aren't really important, disagreeing about what kind of flowers or food should be procured—sometimes a wedding becomes a stage upon which families act out all their long-simmering resentments or unfulfilled fantasies. Otherwise intelligent, rational people often behave in stunningly silly ways around the time of a wedding. Only a very powerful force could cause this kind of temporary insanity.

◇

He was Mister Cool: a successful businessman, marrying a stately and talented woman. The wedding was no big deal to him. They had been living together for years, and it seemed time to make it official. Just a simple ceremony in her parents' back yard, just a few family members and friends, a nice meal afterwards.

I showed up at the house early, and after a while, he drove up in his Porsche. He had just finished a game of racquetball. He hopped out of the car in his shorts and polo shirt. "Guess I'd better freshen up a bit!" he said, with a jaunty air.

We gathered in the back yard—only seven people in attendance, including myself. It was a nice summer day, not hot. The bride and groom came out of the house together and stood in front of me under the arbor. A handsome man, a lovely woman, looking like the perfect couple. As I began speaking, I noticed that he was starting to sweat profusely. Soon, sweat was coming off the end of his nose. First in drops, then in a steady stream. His shirt began to get so soaked with sweat that I could see his chest hairs through the fabric. The little group of family and friends attempted to keep their composure as they witnessed the spectacle of a grown man dissolving before their eyes.

I have never seen a human being sweat like that, before or since.

The spirit of marriage, the force that binds a couple together in love and loyalty, is something more powerful than the ego. The ritual of the wedding invites that spirit to rise up through us, and there is no telling what it will move us to do. It can spin open the spigots that control tears and sweat, no matter how hard our egos try to keep them closed. It can heat up the coolest Mister Cool until he boils over. It is an experience of God that rocks and rolls our bodies and souls.

Whenever people let me know, in word or attitude, that they think an upcoming ritual is "no big deal," I just smile and wait. More often than not, they are shocked at what happens to them during the ceremony. To deny that these rituals really matter is to deny the existence of their own souls. But the more emphatically a person denies its existence, the more creatively the soul asserts itself. A ritual is a consciously planned event that gives expression to a force that might otherwise express itself in unconscious and perhaps undesirable ways.

They had lived together as boyfriend and girlfriend in San Francisco for a long time. They were happy together, and saw no reason to have a wedding. But quite regularly they would get into arguments over trivial issues, and they could not understand why. Neither of them was really that invested in the outcomes of these arguments. The subject matter wasn't even worth the trouble of discussion. They were bewildered by their own annoying behavior; it didn't make any sense.

One evening, after one of these tiffs, they made a discovery. They realized that the reason they were having these fights was that their souls wanted to be married, but they had not done anything about it. They needed a way to express the reality of their relationship, which had matured and grown beyond being just boyfriend and girlfriend. They needed to say and do something that would invoke a deeper kind of commitment between them, and declare and establish the truth about their bond. Their hearts were so frustrated by this unexpressed need that they took it out on each other in arguments about things that didn't matter. "Let's get married!" they said to each other.

For a few minutes, they talked about how to do it. Then they realized their need to do it was so acute that immediate action was necessary. They packed their bags that instant, went to the airport, flew to Las Vegas, and within three hours of their decision, they were saying their vows in a plastic wedding chapel.

He called me after the wedding to tell me what had happened. If the wedding had not been so long overdue, he said, they would have had me perform the service. I told him their story was so wonderful that even a Las Vegas wedding was made holy by it.

We blessed their marriage after the fact with a bottle of champagne and a nice meal. They had brought a little tape recorder with them to Las Vegas to record their ceremony. So we sat at the dinner table as they replayed it, and listened with delight.

Christian rituals, in their traditional forms, still have great power for traditional believers. But creativity is needed in shaping Christian rituals for the sensibilities of the great majority of people who don't go to church on Sunday. Rituals do not need to include a statement of orthodox faith to be Christian. Most of the ceremonies I perform are for people who do not belong to any church. They really want the ritual, but they don't want it to include theology that doesn't make sense to them.

Most people recognize the spiritual dimension of life. But if traditional Christianity isn't their path, it doesn't seem right for them to have traditional theology included in the ceremony. I tell them we don't have to include the name of Christ in the ceremony; the Christ will be there anyway.

The rite of infant baptism is an ancient Christian practice that I perform in different ways depending on the kind of language that makes sense to the baby's family. It is just as Christian without the words "in the name of the Father, Son, and Holy Ghost" at the moment of baptism. When I use nontraditional words to offer the blessing and mark the child's forehead with water, the Christ is still present. What could be more Christian than "christening" a child with water—as Jesus himself was baptized with water—even if the more arcane theological formulas are left out of the service?

The fact that I am asked to perform nontraditional ceremonies, and even to bless a Las Vegas wedding after the fact, is a very hopeful sign. It means that people seek a connection with Christianity. They find value in it, even if they can't accept all its traditions and doctrines. And my hope is that my willingness to do and tailor these ceremonies is a sign to them that part of the church is willing to meet them where they are. I hope it's a sign that Christianity can evolve beyond orthodoxy, and make the transformative power of ritual available to many more people.

21

Bread and Wine: Symbol and Reality

Jan and David, longtime and faithful members of College Heights Church, volunteered to feed the choir a full-course breakfast on Easter morning. After eating the wonderful meal, the choir went into the sanctuary to begin its practice, and I helped Jan and David wash the dishes. After a little while, the choir members invited the couple to come into the sanctuary and sit in front of them. They began to sing Jan's favorite Easter song, "Feed My Lambs." This was not a song they were performing in worship, but rather one they had decided on the spot to sing to her at this special moment. She burst into tears, and as I watched and listened at the kitchen door, I cried, too.

The choir members were the lambs that she and her family had just fed, and now it was the choir's turn to feed her. In the words of the song, "As ye do unto my flock, thus ye do to Me."

That beautiful moment at church defines "communion" for me. There is a mystical but very real communion of souls that can happen when, with intention, we do what Jesus did with his disciples at the Last Supper. The Christ—the presence of God within and among people—is certainly alive in us when we break bread together, both in the communion ritual and in other special moments like that breakfast on Easter morning. "The bread that we break, is it not a sharing in the body of Christ? Because there is one bread, we who are many are one body, for we all partake of the one bread." (1 Corinthians 10:16-17)

We are more than just our individual bodies. We are part of a larger body that includes everyone in our communion circle at church, and all people everywhere and in every age. The ritual of communion invites us to let go of our attachments to our separate personalities, and identify instead with the universal body that is the Christ.

How physical must love become in order for us to know and trust it? The story of "doubting" Thomas, the disciple who would not believe that Jesus had really risen from the dead until he was able to touch the wounds in his hands and side (John 20:24-25), illustrates this question. And so does that universal experience of new lovers. Are words and longing gazes enough, or does it take a passionate embrace to prove that love is real? There is a movement between the spiritual and the physical which love keeps in constant and sometimes tantalizing tension.

Just how physical is the love that is the Christ? Are bread and wine just symbolic, or are they Jesus in flesh and blood? Some of the greatest struggles of the Protestant Reformation centered on this question. Martin Luther, whose followers to this day maintain much of the Catholic ritual of the Mass, vehemently refuted the arguments of Huldreich Zwingli, one of the founders of Reformed Protestantism. Zwingli claimed that the blessed elements of bread and wine were symbols, and not the real flesh and blood of Jesus. Luther claimed that they were both bread and body, wine and blood.

From our vantage point, 500 years later, this dispute might seem downright silly. But at the time, it had great philosophical and even political significance. There is still a split within traditional Christianity—generally between the Catholics and Lutherans on one side, and Reformed Protestants on the other— over the nature of the bread and wine in the Lord's Supper.

I do not believe that the bread and wine become the physical body and blood of the historical Jesus when they are blessed in the ritual of the Mass or the Lord's Supper. But there is still great significance in the bread and wine, and it is more than symbolic. The ritual of bread and wine presents a healthy challenge to our modern way of thinking about reality.

To make sense of the Eucharist we need to reflect on the nature of symbol and reality. In our culture today, we see a difference between symbols and that to which they refer. A word is a symbol that stands for something else. There is usually very little intrinsic connection between the word and its referent. For instance, the printed word "wine" does not look like wine, nor does the spoken word "wine" sound like wine being poured out of a bottle. There is nothing about the word itself that would suggest that it had anything to do with the object to which it refers. We tend to think of wine itself as something real, and the word "wine" as something symbolic.

In the ancient world, and well past the biblical era, this was not the case. Until rather recently in history, people thought of words as being powerful entities with lives of their own. Words were understood to have a sort of power over that to which they referred. They were understood to share in the reality of the things to which they pointed. For this reason, the power of naming was considered God-like. The Genesis story says that after creating all the animals, God brought them to Adam to see what he would name them (Genesis 2:18-19). This was a sign that God had given Adam dominion over all the creatures of the earth (Genesis 1:26).

The tangible nature of words in the ancient world helps to make sense of Isaiah 55:10-11, in which God speaks: "For as the rain and the snow come down from heaven, and do not return there until they have watered the earth, making it bring forth and sprout, giving seed to the sower and bread to the eater, so shall my word be that goes out from my mouth; it shall not return to me empty, but it shall accomplish that which I purpose, and succeed in the thing for which I sent it." These were more than metaphors for Isaiah's audience. People truly believed that words were real things that went forth from their mouths and then had lives all their own, doing things on behalf of the person who spoke them.

Another example of this understanding of the nature of words appears in the story of Isaac's blessing of Jacob. When he found out that he had made a mistake and had given his inheritance to the wrong son, it was too late. The words had gone forth out of his mouth, and there could be no taking them back.

The power of the word was so great that the Jewish people did not speak God's name, because to do so would be blasphemy. The name of God was not just a symbol representing God. It *was* God. God's personal name, Yahweh, was probably an ancient form of the verb "to be." Hence the answer when Abraham asked the identity of the burning bush that spoke to him in the wilderness: "I AM." God's name was the same as God's being. So instead of pronouncing the name "Yahweh" when its consonants YHWH appeared in the text of the Old Testament Scriptures, the Jews used the words "Lord" or "God" in its place. The opening verse of the gospel of John, "In the beginning was the Word," suggests an active, creative power rather than a mere symbol. The Christian mystical tradition understands that the name of Jesus Christ is itself holy. To experience the divine name in prayer or chanting is to experience God.

A similar situation exists in the Hindu tradition. The "OM" is no mere name for God: it *is* God. When Hindus chant the OM, the bodily vibrations of the chant itself are sacred. The sound of the OM itself can establish mystical union with God.

Until the Reformation era, libraries were noisy places. Even in private, monks read Scripture and other texts out loud, out of an implicit respect for the potency of words. Words weren't just ideas; they were physical things that manifested through the physical act of speaking.

Our culture has lost this sense of the power of words. There are many reasons for this change, not the least of which was the sharp rise in the general public's literacy that occurred due to the emergence of the printing press during the Reformation era. If *anybody* could read, there was nothing quite so special or sacred about the written word anymore. And as more and more words were printed, the power of the spoken word diminished. Perhaps Luther's fierce denunciation of Zwingli was a gut-level reaction to this impending loss. Luther must have known that if symbols were separated from the things to which they referred, the human soul would become increasingly alienated from the world.

Money is another good example of this process of separation of symbol from referent. First, there were gold coins: the gold itself was the object of value. Then there were printed paper notes that were redeemable for a certain amount of gold. Then the paper notes became valuable in themselves. Then written accounts symbolized paper notes. Then computer codes symbolized the written accounts.

Today, a dollar is completely alienated from its original intrinsic meaning. A dollar isn't worth a fixed amount of gold anymore. It might be worth 10 minutes of labor at a fast-food restaurant, or it might be worth a candy bar, or it might be worth bus fare across town. But there is nothing, anywhere, that is permanently dollar-like except that piece of paper you carry in your wallet, a strip of pressed and printed fibers which intrinsically is worth next to nothing.

There are huge numbers of business people who do nothing but manipulate symbols such as words and money, and often these people are utterly divorced from any kind of connection with the referents of those symbols. The money they manage has no intrinsic connection with the goods and services it represents. It is no wonder that Jesus said, "You cannot serve both God and wealth." (Matthew 6:24) Wealth, or "mammon," becomes an abstraction that can manipulate and be manipulated, resulting in alienation of people from each other and from God.

But the bread and the wine of the Lord's Supper offer a taste of relief from this alienation. They are what they represent. We depend on food for survival; we savor the taste of bread and of wine. We eat the holy meal together in community, upon which we depend for our sanity if not for our physical survival. Much of our eating in everyday life has a sacramental quality: think of the many meals that are more about nourishing interpersonal relationships than they are about ingesting vitamins and minerals.

When Jesus blessed the Passover meal he shared with his disciples before his crucifixion, he said, "This is my body. . . . This is my blood . . ." (Mark 14:22, 24) What did he mean? That he was in three places at once—his human body, a loaf of unleavened bread, and a cup of wine? Or was he doing what he had done so many times before: shaking up the minds of his disciples with a parable to shock them out of attachment to their egos? In his words, I hear the same sort of message that was implicit in his earlier questioning of his disciples: "But who do you say that I am?" (Mark 8:29) He was challenging them to experience God directly, to get past their assumption that his life, and theirs, was only about the body and the personality. "This is my body. . . . This is my blood . . ." When I read this passage, I hear him saying: "As you partake of this bread and wine, join me in partaking of my true Self, which is God. Let your hunger and thirst for God be satisfied as we share this meal among us in loving community."

When I experience God, I notice a change in my relationship to all things. I'm no longer alienated from the world around me. I was meditating recently with students in Stanford University's magnificent Memorial Church. We sat silent, bathed in the beautiful light streaming through the stained glass windows of the cupola. Outside, an air compressor started rumbling as construction workers began their job. At first the sound was annoying. "When will all this construction stop, so we can meditate in peace and quiet?" I silently fumed. But after meditating for about half an hour, I was startled to notice that the sound was no longer coming from something and somewhere else. It was coming from me. Not the "me" that thinks of himself as the particular personality symbolized by my name, but rather the "me" that is God existing in and through all things, including air compressors. In the divine context, that sound and I became one; while in the everyday context, my body and the source of the sound continued to be distinct.

In a similar vein, I notice that when my heart opens to another person, it is as if we are one. Yet at the same time, our individuality remains intact. The same can happen with bread and wine. When we take them with intention, they become the "you" and the "I" that together are God—yet they remain bread and wine.

The Eucharist is a ritual that breaks down the separation we believe exists between a symbol and that to which the symbol refers. Other religions and cultures have similar rituals. The Japanese tea ceremony is an example. It is about tea, and yet it is about much more than tea. The ceremony symbolizes all sorts of values and aesthetics, but it is also the embodiment of them, as well. It transports the participants out of their usual state of estrangement from the world around them.

The bread and wine are not literally the body and blood of Jesus, but they are more than symbols. The Eucharist—the ritual enactment of the Last Supper—really can bring us together, body and soul.

◇

Robert sat in the back pew every Sunday. His job was to pull the steeple bell rope hanging in the doorway 10 times to mark the beginning of worship. People avoided sitting near him, because he sang the hymns too loudly and very much out of tune. The little white church, built with a pitched wooden floor by a New England shipwright in the 1860s, echoed with his heartfelt off-key singing. He had suffered a head injury when he was a child. He lived with his mother until she died, and then he moved into a board-and-care home not far from the church I attended as a teenager. He felt love and acceptance at the church, even though the members often avoided him or treated him with condescension. With his twisted face and loud voice he would eagerly greet the people who did approach him at coffee hour. Even after long absences from the church during my college days, he always remembered my name and gave me a vigorous handshake when I came back for visits.

One Sunday, when communion was served, the four deacons passed the trays of little crackers and tiny cups of grape juice down the rows of pews. After serving communion, they got up to the front of the sanctuary to put the trays back on the altar. The congregation was hushed, ready to sing the closing communion hymn. The minister was waiting to put the covers back onto the communion trays. Then, abruptly, one of the deacons picked up two trays from the table. She remembered that someone had been forgotten. Without a word, with all eyes focused on her, she walked down the aisle to the back of the church to serve Robert, sitting alone in the rear pew. Then she returned to put the trays back on the altar.

22

Another Way to Pray

He walked down the side aisle of the old, ornate Memorial Church at Stanford with a huge skateboard under his arm. A lanky freshman with a mop of black hair, he sat down on a pad on the floor of the sanctuary with the rest of us. For 45 minutes every Tuesday morning, he kept silence.

After each session, the students and staff people in the prayer and meditation circle shared aloud how their practice was going. Most of us, including myself, reported the usual challenge: resisting the urge to let our mental lists and obsessions take over the whole time of silence. Not so the freshman. Almost every time, he reported sensations of peace and harmony, visions of flowing colors, moments of union with the divine. When it was time to go, our natural-born mystic put on his huge running shoes, picked up his backpack and skateboard, and hunkered off to class with a blissful smile on his face.

Sometimes I get jealous of people like that. My prayer life is not nearly so eventful. I simply sit and observe myself, until I become aware that it is God who is lovingly observing me. This

experience is serene and beautiful, and it has profound consequences for my life. But there is nothing very flashy about it.
The heavens do not part, nor do beings of light swarm around
me, nor does heavenly music put me into ecstasy. I don't do
any talking, and God doesn't do any talking to me. Mostly I
just sit there and occasionally scratch my nose if it starts to itch.

Traditional Christian prayer is typically a formal address to
God. We begin by assuming a physical position denoting that
we are praying. We say something to God, opening and closing
with reverential terms, often using somewhat stilted language.
This sort of prayer certainly has its place, but prayer needs to
be rescued from the straitjacket of formality.

Another road to prayer begins by observing our own normal, everyday behavior. Most of us talk to ourselves quite a bit.
I carry on rather elaborate conversations with myself, sometimes out loud. I do this a lot while driving alone in my car. It is
such a habit that if someone is silently riding in the car with
me, I'll forget they are there and start talking to myself. I catch
myself quickly, and cough or cover my mouth in a vain attempt
to rescue myself from embarrassment. I know I'm in good company: I've seen plenty of other drivers talking or even yelling
to themselves alone in their cars.

We do this because we relate to ourselves as others. Being
able to do so is the very mark of being human. We are able to
relate with other people only because we are able to relate to
ourselves as if we were others, and vice versa. We get angry at
ourselves, we laugh at ourselves, we frustrate ourselves, we
enjoy ourselves. Part of this relationship with ourselves
includes verbal or other forms of communication. It is a healthy
and necessary thing. It is the basis of our ability to pray.

Much of what we say to ourselves amounts to a kind of
prayer. We ask ourselves to do certain things and to refrain
from doing others. We tell ourselves our innermost secrets and
ask ourselves for advice and support. We ask ourselves for forgiveness. Everything we do in traditional Christian verbal
prayer, we already do in our running dialogues with ourselves.

The difference is that in prayer, we are in dialogue not just with our egos and personalities, but with the divinity that is at the center of our souls. In prayer, we are in communication with the Self that is God. In prayer, we can say everything to God that we say to our ego selves. The content of the communication doesn't need to change. What changes is that we are no longer in dialogue only with our limited, mortal, particular personalities. We are in dialogue with the Self that is eternal and present in us and all other beings in the universe. It is a deeper form of communication because it is a deeper Self to whom we are speaking, not because we are using religious language and holding pious poses.

Verbal prayer can simply be straight talk with God in everyday vernacular, telling it like it is in the same language we use for normal conversation. God has no need to hear flowery language. If we have a conscious relationship with God at all, it is one in which no secrets are hid, anyway. The relationship is made holy not by our piety but rather by the nature of the One with whom we are having it.

The way to learn to pray out loud, then, is to start talking to yourself, and keep doing it until you realize you are talking to God. The same practice works in silence. I find that even when I'm quiet, my internal dialogue doesn't stop. It intensifies: in silence, I talk to myself faster than I do out loud. I'm still communicating with myself; but if I wait long enough, and observe this conversation carefully enough, I get to the point where I realize I am silently talking to God, and God is silently and lovingly listening to my every thought and word.

"Now there was a great wind, so strong that it was splitting mountains and breaking rocks in pieces before the Lord, but the Lord was not in the wind; and after the wind an earthquake; but the Lord was not in the earthquake; and after the earthquake a fire, but the Lord was not in the fire; and after the fire a sound of sheer silence. When Elijah heard it, he wrapped his face in his mantle and went out and stood at the entrance to the cave. Then there came a voice to him that said, 'What are

you doing here, Elijah?' " (1 Kings 19:11-13)   Elijah's experience of waiting for the Lord in the cave mirrors my experience
in silent prayer. Even in the cave of my own mind there's a lot
of noise. Winds, earthquakes, and fires rage in my imagination.
But if I keep listening, eventually I will hear the divine silence
itself, lovingly asking me to account for myself: "What are you
doing here?"

When we pray sincerely for other people in their times of
need, or when we pray for peace and justice in the world, we
are talking to God about what is in our hearts and minds. And
the nature of God is to listen to us and to love us. When I pray
in church out loud, I am not asking a remote Supreme Being to
intervene in history and do what I want him to do. I am simply
declaring what I feel and desire. In the process of this communication with God, I am inspired by God's listening love to
search for the real truth about these feelings and desires. How
deep do they go? Am I really willing to do something about
them? Am I willing to take action myself to help others or to
seek peace and justice in the world?

Prayer is a process of refinement. My words and thoughts
and urges are being examined carefully by God. More and
more of my truth is being revealed to me—not all of it pretty,
either. The process of prayer invites me to bring my actions and
my best purposes into alignment. I may be praying for others,
but it is I who will be changed in the process, so that I can
become most helpful to them.

◈

We had a Christmas party at our house for our extended family,
and all the kids were given gingerbread men. My daughter Liz, age
12 at the time, was sitting on the sofa with her cousin Hannah, age
4. I watched them as they played with the gingerbread men. Liz
playfully took one of the gingerbread men and put its face against
her ear, as if listening to it talk. She nodded and smiled and

answered back. Hannah was transfixed. Her eyes widened, her mouth dropped open in awe. Liz saw her reaction and offered the gingerbread man to her. "Here, Hannah. You can listen, too!" Hannah put it against her ear, and with furrowed eyebrows strained to hear its voice. She sat there for a while until her lips began to quiver. Liz embraced Hannah, comforting her in her disppointment . . .

If we are expecting answers to our prayers in plain English, we are setting ourselves up for frustration. My daughter's conversation was really one between herself and her imagination. She was inviting her cousin to have the same sort of conversation, but that was not what Hannah expected. Likewise, people often get frustrated with prayer, finding it to be a one-way relationship. St. Paul addressed this frustration at not knowing how to pray, not knowing what good it will do: "Likewise the Spirit helps us in our weakness; for we do not know how to pray as we ought, but that very Spirit intercedes with sighs too deep for words." (Romans 8:26)

God prays for us. Prayer answers itself.

◈

As a young person, the Lord's Prayer went in one of my ears and out the other. I heard it countless times, knew it by heart, but felt no significance in it. It is only in the past several years that it has begun to take deep root in my soul. More and more, it speaks to me and for me. The prayer of Jesus is becoming my own.

Our Father, who art in heaven. We say "Our Creator" at our church. But neither address captures the soul in the first word of the prayer. Jesus began the prayer in his native language of Aramaic with the word *Abwoon,* or *Abba,* which literally means "Daddy." It is important to remember that in first-century Israel, the relationship between father and son was much closer than it is in our culture today. When the father died, the son took his place as head of the household and continued in the same occupation as the father. In a way that is unfamiliar to most of us today, the son was a social clone of the father. The father and the son were separated by little more than the time between their birthdays.

When Jesus called God "Daddy," he was making a powerful statement about his relationship with God. And we make the same claim when we pray as Jesus taught us.

Hallowed be thy name. While Jesus claims that his real Self is one with God, his Daddy, he also recognizes that Daddy is holy. He claims his spiritual inheritance, his identity with God. But he also recognizes that his self, his personality, is not the God Self. God's name is holy, but my personal name, the one by which my mortal body and ego are recognized by others, is not.

Thy kingdom come, thy will be done, on earth as it is in heaven. Jesus invokes the transformation of the world into the peaceable kingdom. He stakes out heaven on earth. In the first century, a kingdom was not defined by a map. Rather, it existed wherever there was someone who declared allegiance to the king. Jesus declared allegiance to God, and thereby he staked claim to the earth as part of the kingdom of heaven. This part of the prayer is our pledge of allegiance to God, and a declaration of our intention to extend the divine realm on earth by struggling for justice and peace.

Give us this day our daily bread. Jesus taught people that God would provide sustenance for them, day by day. He taught them to trust, to abandon worry. He taught them to believe they had enough. He remembered the story of the manna that fell from heaven—just enough, no more and no less, for a person to survive for a day. He prayed not just for bread for himself, but for "us." The manna didn't fall just on one person, but on all. If anyone hungers, the community hungers. Praying for "daily" bread makes it a daily prayer. It makes the daily means of our bodily survival a means for maintaining a daily relationship with God.

But there is a hint of anxiety in this line. Jesus taught us not to worry about food, but in his prayer he asks God for it, suggesting that if we don't ask, God might forget to provide it. So it is a prayer to relieve anxiety, to calm our fear that we won't have enough.

And forgive us our debts, as we forgive our debtors. This part of the prayer recognizes our propensity to do evil as an inevitable and universal condition of human life, driving us to need daily confession and reconciliation just as much as we require our daily bread. Forgiveness from God happens in the same breath as forgiveness for each other. But perhaps this line could also be read a different way: "Forgive us the same way we forgive you." We need to forgive God for creating a universe that includes evil and suffering. We need to forgive God for creating us with all our imperfections. We need to forgive God for making us separate from God, estranged and alienated from our divine source. Forgiveness is that reunion with God and with each other that we seek in prayer.

And lead us not into temptation, but deliver us from evil, for thine is the kingdom and the power and the glory forever. I am intrigued with this line because it suggests that God might lead us into temptation, so we need to ask God not to do so. But what kind of temptation might that be? Could it be the temptation to play God—to confuse our fallible, mortal egos with the deeper divine Self within us? There is truth in the joke about the difference between a schizophrenic and a saint: the mentally ill person believes that only he is God, while the saint believes that he and everyone else is God.

Perhaps this line means, "Don't let us get so enraptured by your presence that we start pretending that any one of us is the one and only Almighty God—because yours alone is the kingdom and the power and the glory." Jesus himself experienced this temptation when he went into the desert after his baptism. The spirit of God drove him out to the wilderness, and there he was tantalized by the possibility that he could become a superhero. God led him into a situation in which he would be tempted to be someone that he was not. He did not want to go through that temptation again. The beginning of the prayer claims our union with the divine, as sons are united with their fathers, and the end of the prayer makes it clear that none of us can lord it over the others as if one of us were God alone.

The prayer of Jesus pours out our human nature and our human needs. It is respectful, but also blunt and direct. It does not mince words about what it asks and expects in the relationship with God. This is the way to pray: to speak our truth out loud or in silence, to express our fears and desires, to ask for help in being the best people we can be, to commit to creating the peaceable kingdom, and to enjoy the intimate presence of God.

23

Faith and Healing

At the age of 86, any surgery is a risk. She knew it, but she hated not being able to walk. So she took the chance, clear-eyed. The doctors thought it was worthwhile; usually the procedure was successful.

The surgery on her knee went well, and my dear old friend and former parishioner was relieved as she recuperated at her retirement home. But after a few weeks, she got a fever from an infection that had started as a result of the surgery. She slipped into a coma, and was taken to the hospital and put on strong antibiotics.

Finally, she regained consciousness. When I saw her sitting up for the first time in a week, her face glowing, I was convinced she was going to be fine. But she looked into my eyes with a beatific expression and said, "We need to talk about the memorial service." I told her we could talk about it later. Right now, the doctors and her family and friends expected her to recover completely. Speaking softly and sweetly, she didn't even acknowledge my words about the hopefulness of her medical condition. I left her bedside feeling very confident that she would be more mentally alert when I visited the next day, able to comprehend the good news about her recovery.

But by the middle of that night, she was dead. The infection had returned and her body was too weak to fight it. The news shocked me. I thought she was physically healed, but she had the blissful knowledge that her spirit was healed and her life fulfilled. Only after her death did I understand what she had meant. She had known her story was complete, and was ready for me to help plan her memorial service. I was sorry I had not taken her more seriously, but I was comforted by the memory of the love and peace on her face as she talked to me for the last time.

The Christian work of healing is to help people find the fulfillment my elderly friend experienced the day before her death—whether they are dying or not. Christian healing work can take many forms: doctoring and nursing; praying for healing; praying for discernment of how best to be helpful and supportive; listening; and paying attention to the meanings the disease holds for the person suffering from it. Not all of us are called to the technical tasks of medicine. But any of us— friends, family, or even strangers—may be called to the other equally important tasks of healing. We can be healers of whole human beings, even if we cannot be healers of diseased or injured body parts.

Traditional Christianity tends to look at Jesus' healing miracles as proof of his divinity: only the unique Son of God could have done such marvels. The trouble with this argument is that every single person whom Jesus was supposed to have healed is now dead. You might believe that Jesus literally resurrected people, but there is nothing in the Bible or the Christian tradition to suggest that Jesus made them physically immortal. If he raised Lazarus once, why didn't he keep him raised so we could talk to him today, 2,000 years later? Today, doctors raise people from death all the time, with electric shocks to the heart. They are raised for a while, and then eventually they die, like the rest of us. Just as the ability to raise the dead doesn't turn our doctors into gods, the miracle stories in the New Testament don't prove anything about the divinity of Jesus. Nor do these stories suggest that faith will solve all our medical problems. Instead, these stories are about Jesus' mission to help human beings become whole, through life and through death.

We are being healed all the time through a process of death and resurrection. Skin heals when skin cells die and others grow in their place. Most of the cells in our body decay and die, and our organs are healed with replacement cells many times throughout our lives. Likewise, we suffer emotional and spiritual wounds from the moment we are born. Our need for soul-healing begins with our first infant cry. If our souls weren't constantly being healed from within, our emotions would torment us ceaselessly. But there are times when our inner, unconscious healing powers need our outer consciousness to be activated. Sometimes we can do this ourselves; other times we need the help of healers.

Jesus told his disciples to do two things: proclaim the kingdom of God, and heal (Luke 9:2). For him, the two were interwoven. He preached and healed at the same time.

Preaching the gospel is the work of making life complete by sharing the goodness of the stories of our lives. The gospel tells the meaning, purpose, and wonder of the whole life story. The reason the gospel in the Bible rings true is because it is also the story of our lives.

Likewise, healing is the work of making life whole. A healer is not just somebody who fixes a health problem. A healer is somebody who contributes to the discovery of the meaning and purpose in a person's suffering. The relationship between the healer and the sufferer opens the door for both of them to enter the kingdom of God on earth.

Each of Jesus' healing encounters was unique, because each person he helped had a particular story. Some of these encounters seemed effortless for Jesus, while others pained or drained him. Each story illustrated a different need for healing, and a different way to serve as a Christian healer.

◈

The Gerasene man possessed by demons was among the first people to recognize the significance of Jesus' ministry (Luke 8:26-39). When he saw Jesus approaching, the man with demons said, "What have you to do with me, Jesus, Son of the Most High God?" The gospel story suggests that few people knew the deeper nature of Jesus at that point in his career. But the demoniac instantly recognized Jesus' spiritual gift.

Today we would classify the demoniac's condition as mental illness, and most of us would write off his talk as the ranting of a crazy person. But there is great depth of meaning and value in the experience of the mentally ill. If we dishonor that experience, we dishonor the person who has it, and we fail to receive the wisdom it can offer us.

Mental illness reveals a great deal about the inner life of *all* people. In my years of working with the homeless, I had many encounters with severely disturbed people. I was often shocked with their apparent ability to read my mind. They would tell me immediately if I was grumpy or defensive or judgmental, and usually they were right. They acted as healers for me through the hyperawareness that tormented them, yet also gifted them with great insights.

The story tells us that the demons in the man, fearing their destruction, begged Jesus to send them into a herd of swine. Jesus allowed them to enter the pigs, which then ran down a hillside and drowned in a lake. The presence of pigs was an affront to law-abiding Jews, who were forbidden to eat pork. No doubt the pigs were being raised for the consumption of the Roman occupiers of Israel. When the demons entered the pigs and drowned, two cures were accomplished: the man was cured of his mental illness, and Jesus had also worked a cure against the Roman oppression of the Jewish people.

In addition to his other gifts, Jesus was an extraordinarily effective political activist: drowning the pigs was a powerful form of what we might now call "guerilla theater." Many of our physical and emotional ills are caused by injustices that can only be healed by action for economic and political change. It is fine to pray for relief from the economic distress and physical difficulties. But Jesus tells us that our prayers for this particular kind of healing need to be accompanied by vigorous effort to change the social order that causes these injustices.

◈

Jesus said she was asleep, but her family thought she was dead. Jesus touched the hand of Jairus' 12-year-old daughter, told her to get up, and she did. (Luke 8:40-42, 49-56)

Sometimes sleep is the best medicine, for more reasons than one. Asklepius, the mythical first doctor of Greece, invited the sick to sleep in his temple, where he would listen to them mutter in their dreams. From their dreams, which revealed their unconscious processes, he would learn the secrets of how they became ill, and that would tell him the cure for their illnesses.

But sometimes sleep itself is the disease. We may be dead to the world, and not even know it. So much of the time we're just sleepwalking. We react and respond to the world around us, going through the motions of life, doing what is expected, blindly following our routines—but not really living. Sometimes all it takes to awaken to life, to really live again, is a tender touch: the Christ taking us by the hand and playing reveille for our soul.

When we touch each other in this way, we act as divine healers. My church, at its best, serves in this role. Our worship service is a time to reawaken each other to the magic and wonder that is God's gift of life. Once a month in worship, as a way of magnifying our intentions to be healed and to be healers, members come forward to the altar for the ancient Christian ritual of anointing. This literal and figurative touching of the sign of the cross with soothing oil on the forehead brings body and soul together.

◈

She had a constant flow of blood from her womb, a menstrual period that wouldn't end. Blood was the vital life force, a substance of both spiritual and physical power, making this ailment both one of the spirit and one of the body. Menstruating women were ritually untouchable until their periods ended. This woman was untouchable all the time. But boldly she touched the hem of his garment (Luke 8:43-48). He felt some of his power drain from him at her touch. Then he turned, found the source of his sensation, and told her that her faith had made her well.

So often, illnesses isolate us from each other. When we get sick, people may treat us as untouchables. The disease itself presents its own difficulties, but the isolation that comes with it needs healing just as much. Crossing that wall between the well and the ill is itself a powerful act of healing.

Jesus felt power flowing out of him when the woman was healed. There are times when caring for people who are ill becomes an emotional drain. Healers need support. In our church, I have observed that the caretakers of chronically ill people need more of our phone calls, visits, and help than do the people they are nursing.

◈

When Jesus' disciples encountered a man along the road who had been blind since birth, they challenged Jesus to explain whether it was the result of the man's sin or the sins of his parents. Since in the ancient world seeing was considered a volitional, active, and spiritual process, the inability to see was considered to be as much a spiritual as a physical problem. Jesus answered that "he was born blind so that God's works might be revealed in him." (John 9:1-3) Then Jesus spat on the ground and made mud with his saliva, put the mud in the man's eyes, and told him to wash himself in the pool of Siloam. When the man did so, he was able to see for the first time. Ashes to ashes, dust to dust: Jesus healed the man with the same dust from which he was formed.

I make regular pilgrimages to the desert of New Mexico, and have always found the old Spanish colonial churches in that part of the country entrancing. Many of the churches are in bad repair, so an organization has been formed to restore them with the labor of volunteers from the little towns where the churches are located. At first, people used cement to repair the holes in the adobe structures. But this made matters worse. The caustic property of the cement further decomposed the adobe under it. The villagers learned that the best way to patch holes in the adobe walls of the churches was to gather bleached animal bones from the surrounding desert, insert them into the holes, and spread local adobe mud and straw over them. The bone gave structural strength to the patch, and the adobe bonded to it. The buildings needed to be healed with the same substance out of which they were made. So it is with us: we need to be restored to wholeness with integrity. As healers, we help suffering people find out what they are made of, and help them shape that essence into completion.

◇

Peter said he had no silver or gold to offer the lame beggar (Acts 3:1-10). But Peter said he did have one gift—the name of Christ. The Christ is the manifestation of God in the lives of human beings, *giving us dignity, fulfillment, wholeness. In the name of the Christ, Peter told the man to stand up for himself. The lame man felt a surge of divine power rush through him, into his legs and ankles, and he leaped up immediately.*

We need healing from all that prevents us from standing up on our own, be it physical illness that restricts bodily mobility, or emotional and spiritual conditions that restrict the soul's activity and growth. We need healing from social conditions like poverty or homelessness or racism or sexism that make us feel like second-class people, less than others, unable to stand on a level with everyone else.

◈

To make sense of Christian traditions around healing, it is essential to know that in first-century Palestine, diseases were taken personally. That is, the *person* was ill—not just the body. Blindness and leprosy were considered manifestations of sin, which was a broken relationship with one's self and others and God. From the point of view of the people who knew Jesus, the healings he facilitated were moments of forgiveness and of *personal*, moral redemption. In these moments, people were made whole—not just made healthy, or cured of specific problems. They were completed, restored to appropriate, full relationships with the people and the world around them.

This does not mean they were made invulnerable to the inevitable processes of decay and death; again, none of Jesus' patients are alive today. Jesus' power was not a mere cure for disease. Rather, it was a way for people with broken bodies, souls, and relationships to become whole human beings.

In hospitals today, we have doctors who do medicine and chaplains who do religion. But in the gospel legends of healing, Jesus didn't make such distinctions. Sometimes he prayed for people in order to assist their healing. Sometimes he did something physical, like making a mud poultice to heal a person of blindness. Sometimes his involvement was perfunctory; other times it entailed more elaborate procedures.

Some people claim there is medical proof of the effectiveness of prayer on healing. Whether or not this is true, prayer can certainly benefit those who suffer and those who care for them. It enables them to discern the best courses of thought and action. Is the goal of healing a medical cure and recovery from disease? Or to prepare for death? Or perhaps the resolution of inner and interpersonal conflicts? Prayer clears the vision of the heart and mind so that the best path of healing may be found. And there is no question in my mind that meditative prayer has a profoundly healthy, calming effect on body and soul.

24

Sacred Spaces

When she got to Camp Cazadero, our church conference's summer camp, she was surprised to see all the cars in the gravel parking lot. She got out of her car and walked down the hill to our cabin. We greeted her with hugs and smiles. "So good to see you! But why are you here?"

It had been a bad week for this young woman, a former camper from a few years past. She had boyfriend trouble, she'd just been diagnosed with diabetes, her job wasn't working out, her car had died, and she couldn't figure out whether or not to go back to college. She felt lost and confused and upset. Searching her soul for comfort, the answer finally came: go to Vesper Point at Camp Cazadero. She borrowed a car and hit the road the next morning.

When she got to "Caz," she planned to go to the promontory in the woods where the worship service had been held every evening during her many years as a camper. It was the one place she knew she would feel peace and acceptance. But to her surprise, it was senior high week, and all of her old counselors were there to greet her and hug her and give her support. Not until she had spilled her story to half a dozen people she truly trusted did she make her pilgrimage out to that quiet spot among the redwoods and fir trees

*to sit on one of the log benches and gaze at the cross and the
canyon beyond.*

I refer to it as the "edifice complex," that sometimes annoying
habit of churches to resist change of any kind in the sanctuary,
from the paint colors to the precise position of the altar.

But I have come to honor this powerful sentiment among
church members. Sacred space has a logic all its own, quite
apart from the opinions of up-to-date interior designers or
architects. Over time, perhaps over many generations, the people impart the Spirit of God into the space, and it gathers into
its wood and stone a holiness that can be felt even by a new-
comer. It isn't holy because the paint matches the decor; it is
holy because the paint and the decor and even the rust and the
rot are invested with profound meanings for the people who
worship there.

Vesper Point at Camp Cazadero, a clearing in the woods
with simple log benches, will never earn a page in *Architectural
Digest*. But several generations of children and teens have had
their first awakening to the reality of God at this little outdoor
sanctuary, and their experiences have made the spot sacred. It
occupies a vivid place in the imaginations of thousands of
former campers.

The Christian religion has created countless sacred spaces,
many of which evoke holiness even in the hearts of the non-
Christians who enter them. These sanctuaries and shrines and
places of prayer and meditation, however humble or magnificent, are priceless gifts from the church to the rest of the world.

In addition to such formally defined sanctuaries, there are
natural places that are invested with strong spiritual energy by
all the people who have made pilgrimages to them. Sacred
mountains and springs and other notable geological features
can evoke very intense religious experiences. I have my own
sacred geography. Chimney Rock at Ghost Ranch in New Mex-

ico is a very powerful spot for me, as are several spots on the flanks of Mount Tamalpais in Northern California and a certain viewpoint on a dirt road in the Forest of Nisene Marks in the Santa Cruz Mountains. The granite boulders on the top of Kearsarge Pass in the Sierra Nevada, where the words of Jesus in the Sermon on the Mount first rang true in my soul, became altars to God in that moment. I associate these spectacular spots with certain turning points in my life; they mark stages on my life's journey.

With all the churches in this country, America still has a shortage of public sacred spaces. Most church buildings are reserved primarily for the devotional use of the members of their congregations. Fear of vandalism keeps many church doors shut during the week. Most public space is defined by the demands of automobile traffic, which sterilizes the urban environment and makes it unlikely that many places will be able to draw enough spiritual energy to become sacred. A pilgrimage can be made faster by driving a car, but a long pedestrian approach is part of what makes a place holy. Procession, circumambulation: these movements are vital to invest a space with religious energy. The entry into a sacred space needs to evoke intentionality on the part of the pilgrim. There is a dramatic difference between spaces defined by cars and spaces defined by walking human beings. The lack of a pedestrian culture in many American cities is a major cause for the absence of truly public sacred environments.

Our relationship with God is very much shaped by the geography and architecture of our physical environments. More humane city planning and city building, and greater devotion to preserving wilderness sanctuaries and other powerful natural places, will bring us closer to God. The spirit of God incarnates in human beings, and also dwells in special ways in certain spots in the world. Whatever we can do to make the establishment and preservation of such spots more likely will go far in making our world a more palpably divine place.

25

The Road to Nadaland

On one of my annual peregrinations in the desert, I drove through the Mojave en route to Joshua Tree National Monument. Near Barstow, on a lonesome highway, I saw a big, lone billboard looming above the greasewood and yucca plants dotting the otherwise barren landscape. It said "NADALAND," followed by a phone number. I assumed that it advertised a real estate office that sold "nada"—nothing—vacant desert land. I was intrigued by this description of the landscape around me. Was it really "nada"? Why was I so drawn to NADALAND?

As I drove south I recalled a diagram written by a Christian mystic, St. John of the Cross, in the fifteenth century. He was a Spanish priest whose writings have become classics of spirituality. The diagram is entitled "The Ascent of Mount Carmel." The path to the top of the mountain is formed by his handwriting, repeating the word "nada" over and over again. The ascent is the renunciation of all that seems good in life. Possessions? Nada. Glory? Nada. Knowledge? Nada . . . Nada . . . Nada . . .

And yet in the great absence of things that is the desert, I find fullness. St. John of the Cross also wrote a poem called

"The Dark Night of the Soul," in which he rapturously embraced a nothingness so complete that it was devoid of God. "One dark night, fired with love's urgent longings—ah, sheer grace!—I went out unseen, my whole house being stilled . . ." Paradoxically, this embrace brought him into union with God.

There is more than one Christian road, and if you follow any of those roads back far enough, you will find a crucial fork. It is the point at which one chooses the *via positiva* or the *via negativa*. These two roads go through very different territories, but both are aimed at the top of the same mountain. At different times in our lives, we may find ourselves on one or another of these paths: they are separate, but they re-connect in various places. The *via positiva* is the way of love and delight, the way that embraces experience and finds God in all things. The *via negativa* is not as bad as it sounds. It is the way to find God in the absence of things—even through God's apparent absence. The *via negativa* is not destructive, and does not devalue the goodness of life and its wonders and pleasures. Instead, it explores the ways in which God may be found without these good things.

The *via negativa* is described in Philippians 2:6-7: "Let the same mind be in you that was in Christ Jesus, who though he was in the form of God, did not regard equality with God as something to be exploited, but emptied himself, taking the form of a slave, being born in human likeness." We exploit our spiritual equality with God when we confuse our mortal egos and personalities with God. In order to share in the experience of the Christ, we need to empty ourselves from over-identification with our possessions, roles, and personal qualities. The *via negativa* is the way of shedding this confusion of our limited egos with our innermost divinity. It is a discipline, a practice, that trains us to prevent anything—even a good thing—from getting in the way of our communion with God.

Jesus practiced both ways. By wandering in the desert alone without food for 40 days, by renouncing a settled lifestyle, by living simply, by rejecting the powerful roles that were thrust upon him by his adoring followers, Jesus followed the *via negativa*. He emptied himself, over and over, to make room for the intimate presence of God in his heart and soul.

But Jesus also practiced the *via positiva*. He embraced the world and its pleasures. He liked being around children. He enjoyed a good party. He accepted lavish comforts when they were offered to him. He found God in the good things and the people around him.

I admire the example of Jesus. There are times when I seek God positively in the thick of activity, delighting in the world and the people around me. And there are times when I seek God by making empty spaces in my life, by refraining from satisfying my ego as if it were all that matters. Spending time in Nadaland purifies my heart and makes room for God. In the desert, I find my true place in the cosmos. In the desert, my body and my ego feel like specks, next to nothing—yet I feel profoundly connected, intimately bound to the grand scenery that surrounds me.

In the movie "Lawrence of Arabia," someone asked the sweat- and dust-caked Lawrence why he liked the desert so much. "Because it's clean," he replied. And that's true. Certainly not in the sense that we think of "clean" when we clean the house (although it's been said of the area near the Nadaland sign that it's where everyone dumped the contents of their vacuum cleaner bags). The desert is clean because it is a powerful metaphor, a visual and visceral experience, of the absence of all that makes human beings proud, hopeful, and comfortable. No cities and buildings to remind us how clever we are. No verdant lands to remind us how we can eat the produce of the earth. No forests to remind us how we can make houses out of wood. The desert harshly invites us to face all that we are not. And when we recognize what we are not, then we can see who we are. The desert is a great mirror into which we can gaze, and if we look long enough, we will see God.

The great desert of the American Southwest is just one kind of Nadaland that can serve as a divine mirror, stripping away attachment to all of our other identities. Sometimes illness, depression, and grief can become Nadalands: harsh opportunities to empty ourselves to make room for the Christ experience. Sometimes the *via negativa* is thrust upon us. A former member of my church who suffered from depression called her affliction "the gift of the dark angel." It became the occasion for a profound spiritual deepening for which she is now grateful.

One of the experiences along the *via negativa* is the absence of God. It is hard for us to avoid thinking of God anthropomorphically. We want God to be like us, only better. We expect our experience of God to feel a certain way. It is shattering when all our conceptions of divinity are swept away. "My God, my God, why have you forsaken me?" asked Jesus on the cross (Matthew 27:46), echoing the Psalmist (Psalm 22:1). The bleakest desert of all is the one in which the God we expected does not appear. This is the "dark night of the soul," and it can go on for what seems an eternity.

The gospel story reveals that this was the ultimate emptying of Jesus. And yet, it was to God that he made his lament about God's absence. This made it the most intimate moment of all. Jesus was stripped of all his ideas about who God was and what God was supposed to be like. Any remaining projections of his own ego and personality onto God were decisively withdrawn. This was the moment of Jesus' death, but the culminating moment of the Christ's life. The gospel myth tells us that this was the moment that secured salvation, that bound together God and humanity. The body and the ego were emptied, even of the idea of God, so that God, who is beyond all our ideas and expectations, could be fully realized in human life.

It is at this point on the *via negativa* that Buddhist and Christian spirituality converge. The goal of Buddhist practice is to empty the self of all its conceptions and expectations. This is pursued through disciplines that deprive the senses in order to break the attachment to the body and the ego. The Buddhist way is not opposed to beauty and pleasure in and of themselves. Rather, it aims to cease our frantic grasping at the world, to get past our assumption that our personalities and bodies are all that we are. This makes room for a supreme spiritual state that is beyond all imagining. Buddhists do not talk about God—not because they are atheists, but because God is indescribable, beyond all words and ideas.

Whether we like it or not, times come in each of our lives when we find ourselves hurtling down the road through Nadaland. Even if it makes sense to resist, and to try with all our might to get back on the *via positiva*, while we are passing through Nadaland we might as well take the opportunity to embrace the emptiness and darkness, let ourselves be liberated from our attachments and our ideas, and make room for God in our hearts.

26

Living on Humility Rock

She was a geology student at Stanford, and on a field expedition she discovered an unusual rock. By its appearance and composition, it seemed completely out of place. It did not belong in the strata and formation in which she found it. So she took it back to her dorm room and put it on the windowsill.

At our campus ministry fellowship meeting, she told us that this rock had become very important to her. "I call it my Humility Rock," she said, "because as a geologist, I can't figure it out. I can't explain it. It reminds me that there are many other things that are beyond my understanding, and yet, like Humility Rock, they exist anyway. Faith is like that for me. I experience it, I know it is real, but I cannot explain it. There is a reality bigger and more mysterious than I can comprehend!"

Jesus practiced the spiritual discipline of humility. And "practice" implies that it didn't always come easily for him, any more than it does for the rest of us. There were times when he seemed prideful and arrogant. But he knew better, and consciously exercised the discipline of being humble.

"The Son of Man came not to be served but to serve . . ."
(Mark 10:45)   In words and deeds, Jesus often acted as servant rather than as master of his followers, who were bothered
by his reversal of the role they expected him to play in their
lives. The biblical portrayal of Jesus as a humble servant is
striking, and has been held up as a model of Christian living.
An enormous army of saints, both famous and unknown, has
followed Jesus' example in countless acts of selfless service
throughout the centuries, and is a priceless legacy of the
Christian religion.

But being a humble servant is not as simple as it sounds.
I stumbled into its pitfalls on the road of trying to be caring
and helpful to homeless people and others in crisis. When I
was director of the Urban Ministry of Palo Alto, I was constantly challenged to stay aware of my own need to be needed,
my own ego-driven urge to be the humblest servant of all. My
perverse need to be helpful, combined with another person's
perverse urge to be helpless, could become a recipe for disaster. We could lock ourselves into a cycle of dependence and co-
dependence that could drag both of us down. I learned that
I needed to be humble about being humble. I needed to recognize the limits in a helping relationship, to refrain from acting
as a servant at those critical moments when people really
needed to help themselves through their own God-given
power.

The biblical stories of Jesus' work as a healer include some
helpful examples of this kind of humility. Sometimes people
would ask Jesus for healing, the healing would happen, and
they would thank him—and he would not claim the credit,
recognizing that it was their own faith that had made them
well. They needed to know, and fully appreciate, the inner
power God had already given them to make changes in their
lives. Sometimes the humble servant's job is just to get out of
the way, perhaps offer a bit of encouragement, and let positive
change happen on its own. And other times, with quiet grace
and kindness, it is appropriate to do for others what they cannot do for themselves.

◇

While traditional Christianity has taught us to be humble servants like Jesus, it has not taught us to be humble about our religious convictions.

One day, when I was working at the Urban Ministry's drop-in center, I was approached by a young man who was volunteering with us. He was on the staff of a very large evangelical church in our area. His behavior modeled that of Jesus: he was a "humble servant" for the dozens of homeless people who came to the drop-in center every morning. I was delighted that he had chosen to work with us; he was a valuable member of our team.

But on this morning, I could see that something was troubling him. He came to me and said, "I have been volunteering here for a while, and I love working here. I think this place does vital work, and I really support what happens here. Except for one thing. There is no effort to impart Christ to these people."

We had a stated policy against proselytizing at the drop-in center, although it was perfectly okay for volunteers to share their faith, whatever it was, with the clients. We didn't want people to hide their religion; after all, we were a ministry supported by churches and synagogues, and faith was at the core of all our work. But we couldn't allow our drop-in center to be known as a place where people would be preached at or otherwise urged to convert to any particular religion. This bothered the young man, who felt that urging people to receive Christ was the most important ministry of all.

"It's most interesting that you would bring up this subject on this particular morning," I told him. "If you will turn around, you'll see a gentleman over there who is eating a bowl of oatmeal for breakfast. That man thinks that he is Jesus Christ—actually, he is absolutely certain that he is Jesus Christ. So I invite you to go over to him and see if you can convert Christ to Christ! Let me know how it goes, and then we can talk about why we don't allow proselytizing here." The young man looked at me, baffled, then looked at the 6-foot, 6-inch man with a shaved head who was agitatedly talking to himself between spoonfuls of oatmeal. The volunteer walked away, full of food for thought. He never brought the subject up again.

The irony of this story is that through the young man's actions as a caring, compassionate volunteer, he was imparting Christ to everyone around him, whether or not he ever said a word about his religious convictions. And the further irony is that in a sense, the schizophrenic man who believed he was Jesus really was at least representing the Christ. In the words of Jesus: ". . . just as you did to the least of these who are members of my family, you did it to me." (Matthew 25:40) When Jesus healed the sick, he didn't use it as an opportunity to convince the sick to accept him as their personal Lord and Savior. The Christ in him touched the Christ in them, and that was enough.

Some Christians are humble in every way except in their effort to convert other people to Christianity. Their assertion that Christianity is the only true faith for humanity is spectacularly arrogant, but they proselytize with vigor out of a sincere conviction that everyone on earth must believe as they do or face eternal damnation. Christians who claim to have the only right religious formula for everybody else are not honoring Jesus' humility.

Recently I preached on the Ten Commandments at College Heights Church, and someone in our congregation spoke up during the "talk-back" session that follows the sermon. She added her interpretation of the commandment against taking the name of the Lord in vain. "I think it means that you shouldn't be vain about your religion. You shouldn't assume that everybody else ought to have the same faith that you do." It may not have been the meaning of the words of the commandment in Hebrew, but it was a very appropriate understanding of the second commandment in a world where so much strife is generated by religious vanity.

The contemporary Buddhist teacher Thich Nhat Hanh has gently but pointedly challenged Christianity to give up its worst bad habit—the vanity of assuming it is the only right way to God. He makes this request as one with a very deep respect for Jesus and for the Christian religion. As an unusually sympathetic outsider to Christianity, he sees that this attitude of Christian superiority hinders people from experiencing the heart of Christian faith. His argument against Christian exclusivity is simple and powerful: "It doesn't help." And if this or any other doctrine of Christian tradition doesn't help, why keep it? Why let it be a stumbling block in the way of all the treasures of the Christian faith that are truly helpful in encouraging faith and compassion?

Belief that Christianity is the only true religion, that all others are false and lead people astray, has pandered to the vain and prideful dark side of our human nature. Much as we succumb to the vanity of having the fanciest cars and the most up-to-date wardrobes, sometimes we drive and wear our faith in the same way. It's a lot easier to sell your religious product if you can convince yourself that it is the only one that does the job. But we need to ask ourselves why we would want to *sell* it at all. Is the life of faith about converting everyone to Christianity, getting them to subscribe to the beliefs of the church? Or is it about humbly knowing and loving God, as Jesus did?

I have met some fundamental and evangelical Christians who try hard to be humble about their faith. They still believe that Christianity is the only right and true path, and that those who reject it are condemned to hellfire for eternity. And yet they recognize that it is very presumptuous of them, as mere mortals, to zealously declare that this is the case. They really do believe in a God that is bigger than their own understanding, a God that might have more mysteries to reveal than the ones they have been shown so far. They understand that it is not their place to judge the religious convictions of others. That is God's job.

I have a great deal of respect for this disciplined humility. These Christians are sincere in their desire to stay out of God's way and let their faith speak through their example. But their belief in the exclusive truth of Christianity still gets in the way of spiritual communion between them and people of other faiths. There is a big difference between respectful politeness and an open-hearted, open-minded approach to people of other religious beliefs. There is a profound contradiction in claiming to have faith in a God who is greater than our ability to fully comprehend, and at the same time claiming that traditional Christianity is the only true faith in that God.

◈

A man bowed down in front of Jesus and asked, "Good Teacher, what must I do to inherit eternal life?" Jesus said to him, "Why do you call me good? No one is good but God alone." (Mark 10:18)

Jesus, as an ego or a personality, was a teacher, not God. But in his deepest Self, which transcended his ego, he was divine— and that is true for all of us. Similarly, when we call ourselves "Christian," we are merely adorning our egos. We are called to worship God, not Christianity. What is divine is our encounter with God, something that is available to Christians and non-Christians alike.

Traditional Christianity believes that it alone has the Christ, but we are called to a deeper humility that honors the possibility that anybody can have the Christ experience, whether or not they are Christians. All of us live on a Humility Rock called earth, a place that was created by a Power beyond our understanding. Humble acts of service are outward manifestations of an inner awareness that our egos—including our religious identities—are ephemeral and mortal, but our innermost Selves are one in Christ.

27

Another Rule:
From Golden to Diamond

I cried for half an hour, solid, once I figured out what it was.

I had told my wife, Roberta, about my sweetest memory of my father. When I was a kid, I loved to collect rocks. Indeed, to this day, when I'm out on the road in the desert, I feel compelled to step on the brakes at road cuts, pull off to the side, and poke around for crystals or fossils. When I was about 10 years old, my dad built me a little cubicle under the basement stairs, framed it with wood and covered it with chicken wire—no doubt so he could see through it and keep an eye on me. It had a table and shelves for keeping my rocks and fossils. I put a misspelled sign on the door: "Meuseum." Whenever I think of it, I feel my father's love and care for me, his ability to step outside himself.

Roberta was inspired by this story to organize one of the most wonderful presents I have ever received. She enlisted the help of my dad and my brother-in-law, and they built a little cabinet that was shaped inside just like the underside of a stairway, put chicken wire doors on it, and mounted it in our house while I was at work, just before Christmas. On one of the doors, Roberta hung a smooth little rock with the word "Meuseum" written on it.

When I got home, she showed it to me, with a beatific smile on her face. I stared at it dumbly for a little while, not having a clue what it was. Then I saw the rock, opened the chicken wire doors, saw the shape of the stairwell inside, and a flood of emotion swept over me.

"Do unto others as you would have them do to you." (Luke 6:31)   Surely this is one of the most basic Christian principles for living, one of the most frequently quoted passages from the Bible.

But the Scriptures need to be taken with a grain of salt—or perhaps with a grain of diamond. A literal interpretation can lead to absurdities or, worse, to unholy and inhumane conclusions. I search deeper than the surface for meaning in Bible stories such as the virgin birth and the resurrection. But I am surprised to find that even Jesus' "Golden Rule" must be taken at more than face value to make practical sense.

Do unto others as you would have them do to you. This quote from Jesus has found a cherished place in our civilization, quite apart from Christianity. It is a maxim that guides people in everyday relationships around the globe, because phrases similar to it are to be found in all the major religions and cultures. But to achieve its intent, we'll need to find the diamond that is embedded in the Golden Rule like a jewel in a ring.

I have learned—the hard way, as usual—that many people do not want to be "done unto" the way I wish to be "done unto." For instance, I like people to communicate with me in a direct, blunt, honest manner. But many people don't like it at all when I communicate with them that way. They want me to be more discreet and roundabout in my expressions, and they want me to soften my language with euphemisms and hints.

I've learned that there are many situations in which I can give people what they want, the way they want it, and still remain true to myself and my own needs. Why not do unto them the way they want it to be done, even if it is not the way I want them to do unto me? I don't need to do it my way all the time. I have learned that it is often best for me to do unto others in a way very different than I would have them do unto me. After all, I also prefer other people to give it to me my way, even if it is different from the way they would want to be treated themselves.

My wife had absolutely no use for a cabinet shaped like the underside of a basement staircase and covered with chicken wire. But she gave it to me, and even allowed it to hang on a wall in our home, knowing that what might be junk to her would be an incredible treasure to me. I have a healthy jealousy of her ability to take that marvelous step beyond the literal meaning of the Golden Rule.

A friend of mine came up with this rule: "Do unto others as they would have you do unto them." I call it the Diamond Rule. It is a natural consequence of Jesus' Golden Rule, a corollary to it. To practice the Diamond Rule is to take a step outside our ego selves, to try to discern and respond to the unique needs of the people around us—needs that may differ greatly from our own. It's a step that brings us closer to the divine love that Jesus preached and practiced.

28

Another Road
to Soulful Sexuality

There were two little plastic grooms standing next to each other on top of the frosting. Yes, it was jarring at first for the people gathering at College Heights Church to bless the commitment of two men to love each other and to be loyal to each other for the rest of their lives. Few people in attendance had seen that kind of wedding cake decoration before. While the families of both of the men loved them dearly, and had long ago learned to accept their sexual orientation, they showed some trepidation as the reality of the event became apparent to them. They felt that they were crossing uncharted waters.

It was my first time officiating at the holy union of a gay couple. But in my meetings with the men before the event, I was profoundly moved by the depth of their commitment, the warmth and caring in their relationship, and the unmistakable similarity of it to heterosexual marriage at its best. The delights and challenges of their commitment were hardly different from those of any heterosexual couple I have counseled. One of the men had grown up in our church, and it meant a great deal to him for the *service to happen at College Heights. I felt honored to be asked to give the church's blessing to this beautiful relationship.*

As the crowd gathered, and as we stood in the front of the sanctuary to begin the ceremony, I felt a collective sigh of relief and recognition in the congregation. There wasn't anything very unusual about this event, after all. It was a wedding: an invocation of the power of God that had transformed a romance into a lasting bond with a higher purpose. The initial trepidation melted away, and as always happens at weddings, eyes filled with loving and joyful tears.

It is time to return sexuality, and the enduring bond it creates, to its rightful place at the very heart of Christian spiritual practice. To do so, some old and unhealthy habits of Christian culture must be abandoned.

There are some excellent historical reasons for the negative attitude of early Christianity toward sexuality. Many rules and prohibitions in the Bible about sexual expression made sense in the context of their times. The Old Testament story of Onan is a wonderful case in point. Because Onan refused to impregnate his sister-in-law Tamar, "What he did was displeasing in the sight of the Lord, and he put him to death . . ." (Genesis 38:10)   In a time and place when a high percentage of children died very young, and the survival of your offspring was essential to your own survival in old age, it was no wonder that the effective deposition of every last sperm in every appropriate womb was a heavy social and religious obligation. But in a time when the survival of our overpopulated human race depends on limiting the number of pregnancies, the biblical prohibition against "onanism" should rightly be called into question. Our social and religious obligation now calls for making reproductive choice available to everyone.

The Christians of the New Testament era had their own good reasons for rules limiting sexual expression. The church reacted strongly to the sexual abuses and excesses that were commonplace in the Roman era. Predatory sexuality was rampant, with rape and incest the norm in many households. There was no recourse for slaves abused by masters or children abused by parents and relatives. Homosexual rape was common. In the midst of this nightmare, Christianity emerged as an alternative sexual culture that encouraged abstinence, or at least restraint and modesty within the bounds of sanctioned marriage.

The Christian approach was morally inviting in that time of outrageous sexual violence. Christian prohibitions against homosexuality were made in the context of a society in which it was common for men to rape young boys. Proscribing all homosexual relationships was an understandable reaction to the climate of abuse at that time. But if we fast-forward 2,000 years, and we see loving, committed, homosexual relationships that deserve to be celebrated by the church, we also see that today those proscriptions may be inapplicable and hurtful.

Sex keeps body and soul together. It binds human beings together in relationships that can bring them indescribably close to each other and to God. It is time for Christianity to take another road, honoring sexuality as an expression of faith, deepening and enriching it.

Lovemaking is a sacred act. In order for sexual relations to become true lovemaking, time, trust, respect, care, and disciplined sensitivity are necessary. There is simply no comparison between a sex act of people who don't really want to know or care about each other, and the eruption of bliss between people who have bonded with each other at many levels and are completely open to each other emotionally, spiritually, and physically. The bed of couples with this kind of relationship is as holy as any church sanctuary. It is this sacredness of lovemaking, evoked through trust, that makes it so gloriously ecstatic and satisfying. Sex is a religious experience, a mystical union that transcends the simple physical mechanics. True lovers step outside their personalities, enter into each other's experience, and treasure each other's souls. Lovemaking is a form of active prayer, focusing on the divine presence in each other.

Sacred lovemaking is not confined to the traditional structures of marriage, although it is very likely to result in that kind of committed relationship. Most of the good marriages I have witnessed started with beautiful, healthy, premarital sexual relationships, although there are many other wonderful marriages in which lovemaking happened only after the ceremony. And there are occasions when a caring and meaningful sexual relationship can happen for a short period of time for single people. If there are no other partners whose trust could be violated, if there is genuine care for and protection of each other, if hearts will be enriched and not broken if the relationship ends, then it is very possible that such a short sexual encounter can be a sacred experience while it lasts. Secrets, lies, broken promises, and carelessness may make a sexual relationship seem exciting, but they get in the way of the most fulfilling kind of sex in both the short and the long term.

Christianity can best promote healthy sex by celebrating soulful lovemaking rather than by preaching a traditional set of rules that made sense only in bygone days. The church can help make sex more humane and more divine by celebrating true lovemaking in a variety of healthy sexual relationships. The faith offers rich images and rituals that can contribute to a heightened appreciation of sex and of other sensual experiences.

Jesus washed the feet of his disciples at the Last Supper. At College Heights Church, this provides a cherished moment in our Maundy Thursday ritual during Holy Week. Taking the example of Jesus, I wash the feet of our church members, cleansing them with warm water and lemon juice. My wife, taking the role of the woman who massaged Jesus' feet with her hair (Luke 7:38), follows behind me and massages their feet thoroughly with oil. The foot-washing ritual reminds us that our sensuality is inseparable from our experience of the love that is God.

◈

An erotic love poem in the Bible? In antiquity, there were debates within Judaism and Christianity about whether or not the Song of Solomon (also called the "Song of Songs") should be in the canon of Scripture. Many modern biblical commentaries interpret the Song of Solomon in any way but the obvious: a man and a woman inflamed with lusty love for each other.

Over the centuries, embarrassed Jews and Christians have tried to make this poem into an allegory about Yahweh's love for Israel, or Christ's love for the church, or God's love for humanity. They have tried to make it a moralization about the sanctity of marriage—a stretch, since it is not obvious at all in the Song of Songs that the man and the woman are married. The Song is about a pair of lovers who are visiting each other's homes and enjoying passionate sex.

In ancient Western civilization, people weren't labeled as heterosexual or homosexual. Some had sex with the same sex most or all of the time; some had sex with the opposite sex most or all of the time. The Victorian era brought us rigid categories. Now, instead of having "people who sometimes or always express their sexuality with members of the same sex," we have a category of people called "homosexuals." Once we label them as such, we think we know what they are like and what they want. But sexuality is a much more complicated thing, a spectrum full of shades and gradations of preferences.

As Adam named the animals in the Garden of Eden, we name things so we can establish dominion over them. Unfortunately, this naming and controlling can extinguish the wonder of God's gift of sexuality as it is so delightfully described in the Song of Solomon. The man and the woman in this poem are not categorizing and managing their sexuality. Rather, they are elevating it to a high plane, exalting it, lingering over it, enjoying it. They don't give cold Latin names to their sexual identities, organs, or acts, as if they were biological phenomena to study.

Instead, they describe each other as a "gazelle" or as a "shorn ewe." Their erotic allusions include "clusters" of dates or grapes. They describe their experience as "a garden fountain, a well of living water, and flowing streams from Lebanon." (Song of Solomon 4:15)

I find poetry to be a much more accurate and evocative way of describing sexuality than movies or photographs. Lovemaking is poetry; it is about the way it feels, not just about seeing. And poetry is not something that you manage and control. It is an out-of-ego experience. The Holy Spirit expresses poetry through our sexuality.

In the gospels, we read that when the Holy Spirit came to Jesus at his baptism in the River Jordan, it descended upon him like a dove. Nothing but that kind of poetry would do any justice to such an ecstatic subjective experience. Likewise, in the Song of Solomon, the reader feels the transcendent climactic moment of love as the poetic gazelles suddenly, silently, and gracefully bound away into the air, prancing effortlessly up hillsides of soft grass.

Sex is channeled through the body, but it is essentially spiritual. We need sex education in our schools to teach the mechanics of the body, and we need sense education in our communities of faith to teach that lovemaking celebrates the divine in each other.

29

The Practice of Beauty

I heard a thumping sound outside, so I opened the back door of the church. There stood a man I'd never seen before: a man with a wide smile and a twinkle in his eyes behind thick glasses; a spare man with a salt-and-pepper beard and a cane in one hand. Slowly he mouthed what seemed to be the words of a request to come inside, which I immediately invited him to do.

With the hand that worked, he held out his Iranian passport, and he showed me a notebook which indicated his nearby residence address at a board-and-care home for disabled seniors. He looked out the windows from the sanctuary, gazing into the bright air with the whole bay and the distant hills in clear view, and said his first recognizable words: "Beautiful, beautiful." He saw the picture of Jesus on the wall and, with a prayerful expression, said "Beautiful, beautiful." He pointed at Jesus, then looked upwards and said "Allah!" I nodded vigorously. Without saying anything else, he and I worshipped the One God together. Tilting his head back, smiling, shaking his head, he seemed to be enraptured with the beauty that he was finding. But nothing in our sanctuary or our view of the bay was as beautiful as this angel who had caught me unaware with the tap of his cane on the door.

Later, he pointed to his head and said, "Stroke. Stroke."
I nodded, as if I could understand. But how could my brain think
in the same way as the part of his brain that was still functional?
His world lay across a Grand Canyon from mine, yet there we
stood, worshipfully enjoying a beautiful day together. A holy spirit
communicated between us with sighs too deep for the words we
could not share.

And as I stood in silence with him, I saw some of the beauty
in the way he saw it. I stopped trying to communicate with him as
I would with people who have not had strokes. And I realized that,
had he not been a stroke patient, so much of what I would have
said would have been chatter, anyway. The souls of most of us are
bobbing along together in a great sea of divine beauty that we
barely notice as we make small talk with each other. But he and I,
denied this distraction, let the beauty carry us along as we slowly
walked together in silence through the sanctuary.

As he was leaving, I wrote down the time of our Sunday
worship in his notebook. "Beautiful, beautiful," he said, waving his
cane, smiling, bowing prayerfully, as he slowly walked away, having
blessed me and our church with a visitation.

One of the many jobs I took to put myself through college
was working as a nursing home orderly. It was one of the most
meaningful forms of ministry I have ever done—and the lowest paying.

One of my patients was a woman in her 80s who had suffered a severe stroke. In the nursing home, an occupational
therapist offered her some art supplies. For the first time in her
life, the elderly woman began to paint, and her work was stunning. The colors glowed; the forms were impressionistic and
wonderfully evocative. The stroke seemed to have cleared a
channel that enabled her to see and express beauty she had

never before known in her life. Despite her deteriorating physical condition, there was an effulgence about her face that was striking. She *was* the beauty that she saw and created.

Spiritual practice is another road, usually less traumatic than having a stroke, to find and appreciate the beauty that surrounds us all the time. The visual, architectural, and musical traditions of Christianity are unfathomably rich. From its earliest days, Christian faith has opened the inner and outer eye to an appreciation of beauty. Christianity helps us *become* the beauty we see.

Greek philosophy put forward the concept of ideal forms, which was woven into ancient cosmology. The outermost heavenly sphere was the realm of ideal forms and ratios. All earthly creations were more or less faithful exemplars of these heavenly relationships of color and shape and sound. Earthly music was an imperfect attempt to reproduce the "music of the spheres," the subtle but glorious vibrations of the crystalline spheres of the heavens moving against each other. It was music that could be heard only through prayerful meditation, an intentional effort to listen for something behind all the background noise of everyday life. Earthly architecture employed heavenly spatial relationships such as the "golden rectangle," which was constructed using the geometrical "divine proportion." A rectangle with a length approximately 1.618 times its width was especially pleasing to the eye, and was considered a divine shape. The art of mathematics, used to determine the ratios in music and design, was received through divine inspiration. Beauty was divine, and the ability of humans to describe it and create it was considered a divine gift.

Christianity inherited this understanding from classical antiquity, but it was in tension with the Semitic sanction against "graven images." There has always been a tension in Christianity between iconography and iconoclasm, between recognizing that God is the source of all beauty and refusing to worship that beauty as if it *were* the One who inspires it. Today, this tension is illustrated by the fact that some Christian churches are adorned with spectacular art while others are stark and plain. Ironically, some austere buildings are examples of the finest architecture, embodying the commitment to simplicity of the congregations that built them. The aesthetic of the fiercely iconoclastic Amish, who don't build church structures at all, is exceptionally lovely. Some of the churches that rejected organs and pianos as being incitements to carnal passion have developed particularly fine *a cappella* singing traditions.

Divine beauty has a way of finding expression throughout Christianity, whether sanctioned consciously or not. This happens because divine beauty is everywhere, and Jesus taught us to have eyes to see and ears to hear. Jesus taught his followers to see a complete meal for 5,000 people in just a handful of loaves and fishes. He taught his followers to consider the beauty of the lilies rather than to focus on all the anxiety-inducing things of this world. He taught his disciples to see the kingdom of God all around them, when others could see only the kingdom of Caesar. Jesus and the early Christians believed that the divine realm of ideal forms had come down to earth. The perfection of heaven was no longer out of the reach of ordinary people. And still today, Jesus' teachings open our inner eyes to see creative possibilities.

Some of the most profoundly Christian art I have ever seen and heard has been produced by people who don't think of themselves as Christians, much less creators of Christian art. I believe that the Christian gospel expresses the universal truth about the relationship of people with God, so I am not at all surprised when I find the themes of the gospel powerfully evoked by non-Christian painters and performers. Even the ecstatic, free-form, improvisational interludes of certain rock concerts have transported me directly into the presence of God.

On the other hand, some of the least inspiring music and art I have encountered has been produced with an intentionally Christian label. Dogmatic correctness does not necessarily make great art, and we need to liberate the church from the limitations of what I might call "Christian formula" art.

Through an appreciation for divine inspiration—conscious or unconscious—the church can make an enormous contribution to creative enterprise, whether or not the sources of the inspiration call themselves Christian.

Our church displays ever-changing shows of "secular" art on the walls of our sanctuary, and our members have developed inner eyes that catch glimmers of the gospel in them. It is not the artist who makes art "Christian." It is the faithful beholder who finds themes and hints of the Christian story in the artist's work, whether or not the artist consciously intended them.

Christianity's enduring artistic contributions are obvious to the outer eyes and ears of anyone who has visited its great cathedrals or listened to its musical classics. But the faith teaches our inner eyes to find loveliness in what outer eyes might once have seen as unlovely. This is one of the most radical original insights of Christianity. Faith takes what we considered shabby earthly copies of the ideal celestial models, and transforms them into divinely perfect ones. The world teaches us to love only that which is beautiful. Our eyes are fed a diet of fashion models' faces on billboards and perfectly muscled men on television every day. But Christianity teaches us to love everyone and everything, no matter how seemingly unlovely, because divine love is the source of all beauty.

The inner eye creates beauty by projecting love out into the world. Christian spiritual practice has trained me to see more and more beauty in the people around me, no matter what shape they're in. The discipline of caring for homeless people, many of them with broken and unwashed bodies, opened me up over time to another way of seeing, hearing, and even smelling them. I began to reinterpret surface appearances and discover the beautiful divine spark in people who once seemed offensive. And as I grow in faith by the grace of God, following the example of Jesus, I see more beauty everywhere else. I'm even more enraptured by clouds, deserts, forests, mountains, and water than I was as a child; but I'm also able to find resonances and symmetries, interplays of color, light, and shadow, in gritty urban environments from which I used to recoil. "Blessed are your eyes, for they see, and your ears, for they hear." (Matthew 13:16)

I can only add a heartfelt "Amen."

PART VI

Open Christianity
as Love in Action

30

Another Road to
Christian Social Activism

I went there often on behalf of the Ecumenical Hunger Program to deliver food boxes to families who had "more month than money." It was an old motel occupied entirely by undocumented families from Mexico and Central America, and it functioned as their permanent housing.

The building was in extremely bad shape. The heaters were unsafe, the plumbing was in bad repair, and there was garbage strewn everywhere. The resident manager was a heavily tattooed methamphetamine user who extorted sex from some of the female tenants in exchange for rent. Many of the one-room units had more than one family living in them; cars parked in front served as extra bedrooms. One evening, as I delivered a food box to one of the units, I was overwhelmed with the sweltering heat of human bodies when the door opened. At least a dozen people called that motel room home.

In response to these conditions, a group of local agencies banded together to help the residents of the motel cope with their substandard housing. We provided emergency food, clothes, and furniture to the most destitute families. A Catholic group provided on-site tutoring and other activities for the children, who were the majority of the residents. Those who became involved in the project began to put pressure on the landlord to improve conditions at the motel, but he refused to make any changes. So pressure was put on the county government to do something.

Bulldozers were the unintended result. The county health department "red-tagged" the motel, declaring it unfit for human habitation. The owner closed the motel and later it was demolished. Two hundred and fifty of the poorest of the poor in the community were left without affordable housing. Had we helped these people or hurt them by focusing attention on the problems at the motel?

That event haunted me when I got involved in a similar project a few years later as director of the Urban Ministry. Our staff became concerned about the future of an old "skid row" single-room occupancy hotel in otherwise upscale downtown Palo Alto. It was in bad shape, and poorly managed. One of the rooms had been turned into a "shooting gallery"—a dope den littered with needles. I had known many of the tenants for years, and was concerned that they might lose their housing. It was just a matter of time before the place would either burn down or be sold.

I contacted the director of the local low-income housing agency about tactics to save the hotel. Together we contacted the owner, who would not consider our proposal to manage or buy the hotel. He later sold it to a private developer who planned to turn it into commercial office space.

We mobilized the residents of the hotel to go to the city council and ask if a way could be found to preserve it. The residents, most of them mentally or physically disabled, met in a downtown church to strategize. Each tenant shared his or her point of view as we sat in the circle. I realized that for most of them, this was their first experience in active citizenship. When the residents spoke at the city council meeting, I was moved to tears. The empowerment that resulted from being meaningfully involved in a public decision-making process which affected their lives transformed them.

In the end, the city changed its general plan and made the preservation of single-room occupancy hotels a priority. A local real estate developer fronted the money for the nonprofit housing agency to buy the hotel from the new owner, and the Urban Ministry turned the "shooting gallery" into an office for a caseworker to assist the residents with their needs. The nonprofit group later took full ownership, rehabilitated the building, added some rooms, and provided a rent subsidy for all the tenants.

In his day, Jesus clearly stood on the side of the poor and dispossessed. He demonstrated compassion toward people suffering from illness or from injustice, declaring that God loves them and calls us to love them, too. Doing something concrete about poverty and powerlessness is integral to the Christian religion.

The story of the Good Samaritan defines this Christian tradition (Luke 10:33). Others ignored the suffering man lying by the side of the road, but the Samaritan—a member of an ethnic group despised by many Jews—was the only one to stop and offer aid. The Samaritan went out of his way to be of service, offering immediate kindness and first aid, and providing the money to keep the wounded man in an inn until he could recover. He didn't just offer a Band-Aid; he offered long-term assistance to help the man regain self-sufficiency.

The Samaritan's response was certainly an example for all of us to emulate. But there's a bigger picture here, suggesting the need for far broader responses, and relating to issues we are all too familiar with today. There was a reason the incident happened in the first place: bandits constantly prowled the road through the desert wilderness from Jerusalem to Jericho. In addition to providing immediate relief for the victim's suffering, there was a need to make the road safer to prevent further incidents. This might have involved engineering a route that avoided places where bandits could hide. It might have involved political work, convincing the government to provide adequate police protection and emergency medical service along the road. It might have involved work for economic justice, so bandits would have means of gainful employment other than thievery.

Some of the most effective actions promoting compassion, peace, and justice don't fall into categories we associate with "service" work. Just as some efforts by do-gooders have negative unintended consequences, many things done for profit (or even for fun!) can have positive unintended consequences for suffering people. The wireless communication industry, as cutthroat a business as any on the planet, has unintentionally created access to crucial information for poor people. In remote areas lacking the grids of telephone wires that would be impossibly expensive for Third World countries to construct and maintain, just a few wireless phones can connect villagers with vital resources around the globe. Who would have thought that the labors of electronic engineers working in cubicles in the First World would be saving lives in the Third World? Lots of wireless phones will be purchased by people who will use them to make life in the First World even more frantic than it already is, furthering the planetary despoliation that harms everyone. But the tiny percentage of wireless phones that comes into the hands of poor rural villagers can have enormous benefits.

Another example of a positive unintended consequence has emerged from one of the chief obstacles to attendance at Sunday worship: golf. Long the bastion of white males who make business deals while on the course, the game itself has forced open these cliques of wealth and power. Golf loses its luster without fresh, skillful players on the greens, even if they don't belong to the elite social class that usually plays the game. One important opportunity for minorities, women, and low-income people to advance their careers and incomes is to learn to swing a club. On the course, they mix as equals with people who have the connections that can get them jobs and financial advice. Who would have thought that offering golf lessons to kids in a low-income neighborhood could be a highly effective anti-poverty program? It is happening in a community near my home, and the young golfers who are in the class will be amazed at the doors that will open to them as a result of taking up the sport.

Given the benefits to poor people of such simple incidents of serendipity, imagine what would happen if we were much more intentional about promoting the cause of social justice through all our activities. It begins by asking questions together about the direct and indirect effects of our way of life on people who are powerless. For example, does the development of the Internet offer more viable economic options to low-income people? Or does it exacerbate the differences among the economic classes, dividing people further into those who have Internet access and those who cannot afford it? What can be done to propagate the good effects, and mitigate the bad effects, of the World Wide Web on the suffering people of the planet? Asking these questions, and answering them with positive actions, can make an enormous difference in the lives of people living in poverty.

I'm a clergyman; it's part of my job to offer personal support and practical help to hurting people. But many compassionate people in industry make contributions of equal or greater value by working hard to direct their enterprises to benefit those who are suffering. If I work hard, I hope to be able to help a few thousand individuals in my lifetime with the personal contact and support I offer as a minister. There's no substitute for this kind of individualized attention. But engineers and business executives in large companies have the opportunity to leverage their efforts to make significant differences in the lives of *millions* of people living in tough circumstances.

Partisan political work can be another profound expression of the compassion that Jesus preached and practiced. A cut in the federal Food Stamp program might amount to a loss of nutrition for poor people that is greater than everything provided by church-based emergency food programs throughout the country. A relatively minor change in the tax code could result in dramatically improved prospects for affordable housing for low-income people, at a scale that overshadows all the heroic efforts of church-based groups like Habitat for Humanity.

Christians are sometimes tempted to put so much energy into charitable relief efforts that we neglect to reform the social structures that perpetuate poverty. If we see the way of the Good Samaritan as the start of a much longer path of Christian service, we can respond much more usefully to the terrible suffering that passes for life for so many people in our world.

Significant work for social justice and peace is rarely rewarded with immediate results. As St. Paul said, "Hope that is seen is not hope. For who hopes for what is seen? But if we hope for what we do not see, we wait for it with patience." (Romans 8:24-25)   These words have been a great comfort to me. Hope for what is not seen is needed to keep striving toward goals that are beyond the reach of any one generation.

It is no accident that some of the greatest social movements in modern times have been led by people of faith. Gandhi's quest to bring India its independence was considered hopeless by many. But his goal was something deeper than mere independence. He believed that the process of achieving self-rule, however long it might take, was a walk of spiritual deepening. Through the independence struggle, more and more truth would be revealed. The British would learn about their real motives and needs, and the Indian people would do the same.

Both would be brought closer to God in the process of the struggle.

Martin Luther King, a student of Gandhi's principles, had the same point of view about the civil rights struggle in the United States. It was not just a political movement. It was a process of spiritual growth for all who were touched by it.

This understanding is at the root of Christian nonviolent action. Jesus told his followers to love their enemies and pray for those who persecuted them (Matthew 5:44). He practiced nonviolent resistance against evil. There is a tradition in Christianity called "code-ethic pacifism" that forswears all forms of violence in all situations, even in self-defense. The Anabaptists and the Quakers have tended in this direction. But there is something deeper in Jesus' teaching than merely an absolute prohibition against violence. It is a recognition that our enemies are still human beings like us. It is a steadfast refusal to demonize even the most threatening and destructive of our brothers and sisters.

Our struggles with our enemies can lead us to new levels of truth about each other. They can help us let go of over-identification with nationality, ethnicity, and political commitments. We are not asked to love our enemies as if they were friends or family—Jesus himself used pretty strong language with his enemies (calling the scribes and Pharisees "whited sepulchres" full of rot and filth, for example, in Matthew 23:27). We are challenged to love them as neighbors, as fellow human beings bound with us in a covenant that crosses all boundaries of race and creed and politics. Violence gets in the way of this loving engagement with our enemies.

But nonviolence does not mean passivity. It means vigorous, sometimes radical action that might even cost us our lives. It is better to be violent as a last resort in the process of a struggle to defend life and liberty than it is to do nothing at all. But the first option, for the followers of Jesus' way of loving enemies, is to establish a dialogue with them through forceful, creative actions that do not threaten human life.

Christianity reveals a deeper reason for engaging in struggles for peace and justice. The goals are worthy in themselves, but the effort involved in achieving them can bring us into closer communion with God. If we value the journey as well as the destination, we can keep working to build the kingdom of God despite the inevitable frustrations we'll encounter. We can hope for what we cannot see, and seek it with patience and persistence.

As a product of the social upheavals of the 60s, and a participant in the movement for social change in that era, I noticed that most people who turned out for the demonstrations—even those who seemed committed to the cause—dropped out when change didn't come quickly. A disproportionate number of those who stuck with the movement were the ones who had some kind of active faith practice, Christian or otherwise. Clearly, something inside allowed them to "keep on keepin' on" despite the lack of tangible results and seemingly insurmountable obstacles. Spiritual discipline enables people to take on tasks that are apparently impossible. There is no visible way to end poverty, homelessness, ethnic hatred, violence, and war in the world. But if we hope for what we do not see, we can work to end these problems anyway.

31

Toward a New Covenant of Love

My friend, the manager of a retail store, immediately hired a homeless recovering drug addict with hepatitis the same day our staff sent him from Urban Ministry to apply for the job. I was amazed my friend would take such a chance; I thought he'd give him an interview, but hardly expected him to hire the man.

That was eight years ago. Today, when I go into the store, I am greeted by the smiling face of this formerly homeless fellow, who is now clean, sober, and healthy. He is my friend's most valuable employee. Customers come into the store specifically because of his friendly and helpful manner.

This was hardly the first nor the last incident in which the manager of the store has saved and changed lives through his role as an employer. He has hired other people on the margins of life, patiently helped them adjust to the demands of the job, and taken special care to accommodate their personal needs. He does it without any shrewd calculation of benefit in return, though his humane policies as an employer have earned him a very happy and loyal staff. He does not think of himself as a do-gooder or *social reformer at all. But he has done profound good, and has reformed society in his corner of the world.*

Wе live by percentages. There is a sales tax percentage on purchases, an income tax percentage, a percentage of the restaurant bill that goes for a tip. We take our percentages of profit, and we pay percentages for commissions. And we give our percentage of time and money to charity.

The noble American habit of giving to good causes and to the church has deep and ancient roots. The biblical practice of the tithe—10 percent of one's income given to the priesthood and for helping the poor—continues to this day as an important Christian principle.

But there is an enormous difference between the tithe of ancient Israel and the percentage given to charity by people today. The biblical tithe was given in the context of a covenant between God and Israel. Our current "tithes" to church and charity are framed in a society that is structured by contracts. A covenant is much different from a contract to exchange goods or services of equal value. It is something far beyond a legally binding agreement of expected outcomes between two parties.

Contracts limit relationships, but the Old Testament covenant was a 100 percent relationship between God and the people of Israel. They were bound to love and serve each other in every thought, word, and deed. The covenant was expressed in the Jewish law and in the biblical accounts of the history of Israel. The Old Testament recounts the ways in which that covenant with God was formed, violated, and revitalized time after time. The tithe was just one part of a complete commitment of the Jews to the well-being of each other and to the love and worship of God.

The Old Testament covenant was between God and Israel, but Christianity extended it to the whole world. When Jesus lifted up the cup of wine at the Last Supper (Mark 14), he declared that it sealed a new covenant. He said he would not drink again of the fruit of the vine until he drank it new in the kingdom of God. That kingdom consists of those people who live in a 100 percent covenant of love with each other and with God.

The kingdom of God is what happens when a store manager hires risky employees because he recognizes that there is something more important than profit percentages. The kingdom of God consists of every relationship—marriage, family, church, friendship—that binds people together in unconditional love and care. The constitution of the kingdom of God is a covenant that transcends the right to "the pursuit of happiness" for individuals. It goes far beyond what any government, nonprofit service organization, or church can accomplish for the common good. Christianity describes this covenant, but you don't have to become a Christian to be part of it. This new covenant, which Jesus proclaimed as he lifted up the cup of wine at the Last Supper, includes the whole human family, binding us together with the love that is God.

The United States is governed by a social contract called the Constitution. Part of the enduring genius of this document is that it applies only to a limited sphere: the relationship between people and their government, the limitations on all forms of political power. The Constitution does not contain the ideals by which people live together in peace and harmony; it only enshrines the ideals of democratic statehood. The rest is between us and God.

For instance, the Constitution does not guarantee each citizen a decent place to live and enough food to eat (although I believe a truly civilized society would want to offer those assurances). To have a truly civilized society, there needs to be a covenant of mutual care among its citizens which follows from a covenant between God and people. It is this living covenant that assures not just political democracy, but economic democracy as well.

Faith inspires us to live as if such a covenant exists. If anyone is hungry, ill-housed, badly educated, or disrespected, our
challenge is to act as if the covenant has been broken and work
to restore it. It demands active citizenship in all spheres of life.
Each of us is responsible for fulfilling the whole covenant, and
for *transcending* the percentages of time and money expected of
us by our social institutions.

32

A Theology of "Enough"

"I just can't sleep at night very well anymore," the older woman told me after she had been volunteering for a while at the Urban Ministry, serving homeless people. "How can I sleep in my nice warm bed while there are so many homeless souls out there, shivering in the cold and wet?"

I have heard this many times in the course of my work, and have squirmed in my own bed more than once asking the same question of myself. Even though I have dedicated my life to being of service in the community and through the church, I still question whether or not I have done enough. Jesus asked his disciples to give up everything, including nice soft beds, in order to follow him in service to the poor and sick. Would he say the same to me today, looking at the way I live? How much should I give to benefit others?

The answer is: *everything*. Faith leads me to live as if I am in covenant with all other human beings, and even with animals and plants. Charity is not just a percentage of one's wealth that one gives to others. It's a way of life that takes others into account, 100 percent. If I give 20 percent of my income to UNICEF to feed hungry children in Third World countries, but spend the other 80 percent without regard to its impact on the human and natural environment, I may create more suffering than I have alleviated—even though others might think I'm extravagantly charitable. The challenge is to use *all* my resources to best contribute to the building of the kingdom of heaven on earth. And in a world as interwoven and complex as ours, this is no trivial exercise.

Making money can be difficult, but giving it away intelligently can be even harder. It is not so simple to distribute donations effectively, or to find ways to volunteer time most usefully. Having managed nonprofit human service agencies, I'm aware of the complexities involved in helping people in poverty. If an aid agency pours too much free food into a hungry nation, and does it carelessly, it can discourage local farmers from producing enough food for the nation to feed itself after the hunger crisis passes. If a local homeless service agency doesn't structure its shelter program carefully, and lets clients stay too long and too comfortably, it can discourage clients from seeking the self-sufficiency that might be possible for them. Or, if the shelter offers stays that are too short and too rule-bound, it can simply waste its clients' time with an ultimately useless program that demeans them and slows their progress toward their goals.

The usefulness of a money donation to a service agency depends a great deal on such details. It is possible to give a charity too much, or not enough. Tiny donations can be important, but sometimes they cost the agency more in record keeping than the amount of the donations themselves. And a huge donation targeted for narrow purposes can skew the management and fund-raising of an organization, making it complicated to maintain steady income and expenses.

The Judeo-Christian tradition has a powerful concept that can be used to sort out the best use of our resources for the common good. It is embodied in the simple word *enough*. The Bible is full of stories that suggest the existence of this thing called *enough*. God created the world in six days, then rested on the seventh. God had done *enough*. If God had created more, it would have been too much—far too complicated and messy. If God had created less, there would have been no human beings, the crown of the creation, made in God's own image.

The Sabbath—the day of rest—is grounded in the idea of sufficiency. When the people of Israel were wandering in the desert after liberation from Egypt, God fed them with manna from heaven. If anybody tried to gather and store more than enough to satisfy their hunger, it would rot away overnight. But on the last day of the week, they could gather an extra supply that would not rot, so they would not have to gather it on the Sabbath (Exodus 16). The Jewish law stipulated that every seventh year, a plot of land should be left fallow to rest. It was a basic soil conservation measure, to ensure that the land was used just enough, and not too much, lest it lose its productivity. And the law also stipulated that after the 49th year—a Sabbath of Sabbath years—there would be a 50th "jubilee" year in which all land holdings would revert to the community for redistribution. It was assumed that after 49 years, land tenancy would have become unfair due to sales of land and uneven inheritances. The jubilee ensured that each family had enough land so that all would have enough food (Leviticus 25).

In his Sermon on the Mount, Jesus preached about *enough*. "Look at the birds of the air; they neither sow nor reap nor gather into barns, and yet your heavenly Father feeds them. Are you not of more value than they?" (Matthew 6:26) When he fed 5,000 people with just a few loaves and fishes, he graphically demonstrated this principle (Mark 6:35-44). To the poor, he preached that despite their worries, they would have *enough*. To the rich, he preached that if they gave up everything they had, they would have *enough*.

Enough is not a word that has a place in the global consumer economy of today. The biblical concept of Sabbath is at odds with the current idea that our standard of living can and should continue to get higher, that we can have ever more and ever better stuff. If we lived by the principle of *enough*, corporate capitalism would collapse in a heartbeat.

Every advertisement we see or hear to the contrary, the fact still remains that there is such a thing as *enough*. If we are not sick or starving or homeless, it is possible for us to feel the reality of *enough*. Neither Scripture nor everyday life defines exactly what *enough* is in every circumstance. *Enough* is a moving target, depending on time, place, and person, but it still exists. There is such a thing as having enough food, enough sex, enough work, and enough leisure. There is such a thing as having a good enough house and a good enough car.

Beyond *enough* is the realm of increasingly grotesque excess. We all know roughly where that point is, much as we try to deny it. When the people of Israel collected the manna that dropped from heaven onto the desert floor, they discovered that if one person gathered a little, it was enough to feed that person, and if another person gathered a lot, it was just enough to feed him or her as well, with nothing left over. The amount of manna you needed and the amount of manna you collected was just enough, but that amount differed for each person. If your most basic needs are met, then you can decide that whatever you have is enough, whether that's a little or a lot.

Enough is a spiritual state of equanimity and deep satisfaction. It's a way of being that is not driven by desire for more. If you feel you already have enough, and more comes to you, you might use it, or you might pass it on to others. If more doesn't come to you, you are serene and unbothered. *Enough* allows you to avoid the attack on the soul that often accompanies material obsession.

This is the way of living that Jesus taught. He was not averse to new pleasures, or even to extravagances. When the woman poured expensive ointment over his head and massaged him with it (John 12:1-8), Jesus was criticized for accepting this luxury that could have been sold for money to give to the poor. He was known for enjoying good food and wine at the parties of well-to-do people, and was criticized for not maintaining an ascetic lifestyle. But Jesus' point about abandoning possessions was not about rejecting pleasures or giving up good new experiences. It was about abandoning anxiety, abandoning the kind of grasping desire that consumes the soul. If you need no more than the shirt on your back and the food in front of you, you are free to identify yourself with God instead of with your possessions or the things you desire.

Having worked for years with people in poverty, I have observed an even worse problem than the unfair distribution of wealth. The reality of starvation and homelessness is overwhelming in many areas of the world. But the most insidious problem is the export of untrammeled material desire. The global mass media machine mesmerizes Third World people into believing they need everything First World people have. Residents in less developed locations who once thought they had enough food and shelter are now being told that life really isn't complete without the products advertised on television. People in low-income American neighborhoods, even those who have steady jobs and secure housing, are often mortally embarrassed by how little they have compared to middle-class folks. The consumer culture has taught them that they are poor.

To think of one's self as poor is to believe that what one has is hopelessly inadequate. For all of us to have enough, we must make sure that the most basic needs of everyone for food and shelter and security are met. At the same time, we need to change the culture of the First World, rejecting the cult of runaway material desire and embracing the theology of *enough*.

The Amish provide us a model of what it would be like to live with simply *enough*. Contrary to stereotypes about them, the Amish are neither opposed to pleasure nor opposed to the new and better things that come with technological progress. Their way of life does change. For instance, they have no trouble with use of the telephone, as long as it doesn't intrude into their households. So they use phone booths that dot their countryside. Nor do they have any objections to padding their horse-drawn buggies with modern plush carpeting. They just don't want to deal with the destructive social and environmental effects that result from using automobiles with the same plush carpeting. Slowly, they do add comforts and conveniences to their lifestyle. The dramatic difference is that they do so without an obsessive, compulsive desire to have more than what they already enjoy. As new things come along, they take a long time to evaluate whether or not those things will do them any good. And they have concluded that the price they would pay in reduced quality of life, if they fully adopted the consumer products and services of the mainstream culture, would be far too high. Since they have a culture that presumes they already have *enough*, it takes a great deal of convincing to get them to make sacrifices to get more. A few decisions they made long ago, most notably to keep themselves off the electrical distribution grid, have insulated them from the desire machine of the mass media.

The Amish don't believe they are poor. And their lifestyle is not based on asceticism or abstinence. Like Jesus, they enjoy the physical pleasures of life and delight in the luxuries they make available to themselves. They live according to a theology of *enough*.

It isn't necessary to move to rural Pennsylvania and take up horse-drawn plowing to emulate the Amish, however. If First World people stop believing what the advertising industry tells them, if we spent vastly less time in front of the television, if we stopped being embarrassed to drive cheap cars and live in modest homes, it would have a dramatically beneficial effect on those Second and Third World people who study everything about us with a mixture of disgust, jealousy, and admiration. If First World people no longer felt compelled to buy the latest clothing fashions, then Third World people wouldn't feel so poor and desperate because they must wear old and cast-off garments. If First World people buy their food from local farmers' markets, then Third World farmers can grow food for their own local markets to feed their neighbors, and won't be forced into peonage working for industrial growers that export to the First World. If middle- class kids don't feel compelled to buy the latest overpriced name-brand shoes, then kids from low-income families won't feel tormented with embarrassment if they wear cheap, sensible shoes as well.

The desire of wealthy and middle-class people for absurd excess is poisoning the hearts of everyone on the planet. The products and services we crave are not necessarily evil. What is evil is our refusal to see that we already have *enough*.

Donations to Church World Service are good investments in the lives of struggling Third World people. Most of us can comfortably afford to donate vastly more to such efforts than we do. But what matters even more is how we spend the money and time that we *don't* donate to good causes. Our way of life and our relationship to the things we consume need to change dramatically in order to make life a lot easier for people around the world. It begins by living as if Jesus were right when he taught that we already have *enough*.

33

The Road to Vocation

The Urban Ministry's drop-in center served dozens of functions in the lives of people on the street, including that of a hair salon. We received donations of haircutting equipment and a mirror and stool. Our volunteer barbers from the streets would get the gear from our staff and plug the clippers into an outdoor socket. People would study the abilities of the volunteer barbers. If they were good, a line of nonpaying customers would form.

One day Earl asked us for the clippers. Our staff hesitated before giving them to him. Earl was a chronic alcoholic with a gravelly voice, and he free-associated in rhythm and blues when he was loaded. Several times, I had "86ed"—evicted—him from the drop-in center for being loud and using abusive language. We knew he was harmless, but he made everyone else uncomfortable and we couldn't tolerate his coming in drunk. This time he seemed quiet and not as drunk as usual. So we gave him the clippers, still wondering how Earl could walk a straight line, much less cut one.

An hour later, I looked over to notice that a line had formed in front of the stool. With confident strokes, a steady hand, and a keen eye, Earl displayed his artistry. Eagerly, one after another, kinky, straight, thin, and thick heads of hair presented themselves to him. Now it was Earl's set of clippers, Earl's pair of scissors, Earl's job. I could see his soul taking its rightful place in the world as he scanned the backs of his customers' hair for uneven spots. At closing time, after giving haircuts to lots of happy people, Earl neatly packed the haircutting gear into its box and returned it to us. He then wandered back out into the streets, talking incomprehensibly to himself.

◈

She worked over 20 years in her profession; but the whole time, she knew it wasn't her real vocation. Bright, creative, in the prime of life, this member of our church knew someday she would have to make a change.

She made a date with herself. By that time, whether or not she had figured out what her vocation really was, she was going to quit her job. She kept the date even though it frightened her to give up the security of that job.

She realized she needed some quiet, unscheduled time. As the early weeks of unemployment rolled by, she was uncomfortable being out of the work routine. She felt lazy and unproductive. But then she noticed she was softening and relaxing. There was a different person underneath the stiff shell of efficiency she had worn all those years as part of her professional image. She needed this time to get to know who she really was, so she could answer the call of her next vocational choice with body and soul.

I have the privilege of spending time with students who are in the process of discerning their vocations. Many of them worked hard to pursue rather narrow goals in order to get admitted to Stanford in the first place. But as they approach graduation, they often begin to question the focused ambitions that propelled them successfully through school. I have heard many students lament that they aimed themselves at careers in science, technology, and business in which their desire to serve others with heart and soul may not be encouraged. How can I be an engineer and do service and ministry work at the same time? Will I work hard and make lots of money as a business manager, then retire early to spend the rest of my life being helpful to people or working for social change? How can I become a lawyer and still exercise my artistic and musical talents? These are cries from the heart that deserve a response.

I also have the privilege of spending time with retired people in my church. It's a major adjustment for them to leave their jobs after long careers that provided them with a stable sense of self and self-worth. Some are delighted to be free of roles that never seemed quite appropriate for them in the first place. Others flounder, not knowing who they are anymore, not knowing what to do with themselves. Still others grieve the loss of their roles for a while, but quickly discover all the other possible uses of their time and talents.

Whether just starting or just retiring from a formal vocation, those most likely to feel fulfilled are those who are actively involved in their communities. If you feel like an important part of your neighborhood, temple, church, or civic organization, it almost doesn't matter what occupation you pursue. Your commitment to your community is your vocation, and your specific job is part of the way you contribute. Quickly you realize that all sorts of vocations are essential to serve your community as a whole. It is important to go through a process of inner spiritual discernment to get clear about your vocation in life. But that process is made much more satisfying and distinct if you belong to a close-knit community.

The scoutmaster of our Boy Scout troop was a very important figure in my childhood. I think of him whenever I remember my small hometown. His love of the wilderness was infectious. He taught us to name and appreciate the different kinds of trees and plants; how to live off the land; and most importantly, how to cooperate with each other. Being the volunteer scoutmaster was his true calling, but his paid vocation was completely different. He ran the town's sheet metal shop, constructing ducts for heating and cooling in a business passed down to him by his father. If sheet metal work had not been the family business, he probably would have chosen some other occupation. But he did not appear to be at all unhappy with his job. It probably wouldn't have mattered much if he had been the town's optometrist, mortician, or baker instead of its metal bender, because the role through which his heart and soul shone would still have been that of scoutmaster. That was the duct through which his unique warmth could flow.

In Guadalajara, Mexico, I once met an elderly woman from the United States who had moved to the expatriate community near Lake Chapala. She told me she had gone there to retire with her husband, a wealthy fellow from New York, expecting to do nothing much more than pour tea at social functions. By chance she befriended a group of Huichol Indians and was invited to visit their remote mountain village. She began spending more and more time there. After her husband died, she became the village medic. Without any formal medical training, having spent her life as a high-society matron, she found herself delivering babies and helping people recover from scorpion stings. There she remained until her own health was too frail to continue in that role. She found a flow of love and followed it upstream until she arrived at the place where her gifts could be most useful.

A vocation is a channel through which divine love moves. It flows different ways in different channels, but the love that is God is the same. Too often we get anxious about our vocational choices and our vocational losses because we have over-identified ourselves with them. The banker can be tempted to think that he *is* a banker—that this role defines the core of his being. The doctor is tempted to think that she *is* a doctor—that the white coat not only covers her body at the clinic, but defines her very essence. Christianity teaches us to get past this kind of over-identification with our professions. Jesus' spiritual discipline included a steadfast refusal to equate himself with the roles people expected him to fulfill. He avoided thinking of himself as a king, political savior, or wonder-working doctor; these roles would stifle love if he identified with them too much. He strove to remember that he was no less than the love that flowed through him.

My vocation as a professional minister is a channel through which I have been able to love in ways that make good use of my gifts. But in addition to doing the things for which I was trained at seminary, a great deal of my time as the minister of a small church is spent making minor repairs on the building, weeding and watering the church garden, and taking care of the church's business affairs. These tasks were not part of my vocational plan. I didn't expect so much of my career to be spent wielding pliers and hoes and piles of paper. But each task enables our church community life to flourish. Changing light bulbs in the sanctuary makes it possible for our members to read the songbooks when we sing at our evening potlucks. Tending the flower garden provides a serene sight that enhances worship for the people of the congregation. Being of service to my community is my highest vocation, regardless of my particular career path.

Being a channel for divine love is everyone's vocation. The specific mode we select to carry out that mission is an important—but secondary—consideration.

34

Ministry by Many:
All Are Called

I held his hand as he lay peacefully on his bed in the hospice ward
of the Veterans' Hospital, his eyes fixed on me, his face vaguely
responding to my words and my tears. When I came to visit the
next day, his bed was empty. He had died that night.

Ollie was the janitor of the church where I once worked as
associate minister in Palo Alto. He was an easy-going, caring, sweet-
natured man who would often bake an extra yam for me for lunch
in the church kitchen, where we would sit together and talk. Often,
when I'd go to see a church member who was in the hospital,
I would discover that Ollie had already visited. He was a volunteer
deacon in his Baptist church. Ollie watched out for the people of
his own church and of our congregation, visiting them in the
hospital, talking to them when they got into any kind of need—
accepting people as they were without telling them what to think
or what to do, without judging them. He had no seminary
education, but he had an innate sensitivity to people that made
him a wonderful minister. "Deacon Wright," as he was known in
his church, lived as though his only goal was to be a loving presence

for the people around him. His religion wasn't complicated; faith wasn't something he believed in, but rather something he lived.

They had their own family, but Ollie and his wife also took in foster kids. Ollie kept track of them and cared for them long after they left his home. He volunteered often at the Ecumenical Hunger Program in East Palo Alto, gathering and distributing donated food. He knew a lot of the people who came to the Hunger Program for assistance, and gave them support and encouragement along with their edibles. He had grown up in poverty in rural Oklahoma, and had lived on the streets of California in his young adulthood before he got clean and sober. He was no stranger to hard times, and people in hard times were not strangers to him.

When I went to visit him earlier in the course of his illness, I asked at the nurse's station where his room was. The nurse said, "Oh, he's down the hall—probably cheering somebody else up!"

Being a professional Christian minister has been a study in contradictions. In social situations with people I meet for the first time, there is a sudden awkwardness in the moment they find out what I do for a living. If they were using off-color language, they stop and apologize. Sometimes they take it as a cue to pour out their life stories and ask for personal advice, turning our conversation into a confessional. Almost always they tell me I don't look, talk, or act like a minister, which I have chosen to accept as a compliment. But they also reveal in those moments that there is a powerful stereotype about how ministers are supposed to look, act, and talk. This stereotype haunts me wherever I go, lurking in the background of my relationships. It is so at odds with my own sense of myself as to be absurd.

I seldom wear clerical garb. I don't use religious jargon if I can avoid it. I'm not the fundamentalist most people automatically seem to assume I am when they learn of my occupation. The gap between who I am and what people expect me to be is wide.

Ministry, for me, is about issues far removed from the stereotypical images of a clergyman. Ministry is being available and present for people throughout the passages of their lives. It's finding and sharing the gospel story in each other's lives, whether or not any traditional Christian language is used in the process. Ministry is finding the face of God in the faces of others, and reflecting that face back to them, mirroring the divine spark that flickers in everyone. Ministry is a quality of loving care that is evidenced in all sorts of relationships.

When Jesus partied with tax collectors and other "sinners," just enjoying their presence without preaching at them, he was doing ministry. When Jesus acted as a physical and spiritual healer, he was doing ministry. When Jesus tried to feed thousands of people with just a few loaves and a few fishes, he was doing ministry, because he was demonstrating his heartfelt concern for them despite his lack of adequate visible food to meet their needs.

Many helping relationships take the client-therapist form, in which the expert provides advice, care, or support. There is a clear boundary between the client and the therapist, established by their contract for the provision of the service. By contrast, ministry is a relationship that is bound by a covenant of love in the context of a community. Ministers and those they serve are available to each other as fellow human beings in ways that are not typical of many other helper-client relationships. It is *personal* service, and not only in the sense of politeness or attentiveness.

It's no accident that "parson," an antique word for minister, is a variant of the word "person." The minister's job is to be a person for and with other persons. It is a relationship of "compassion," sharing the passions of people, as they share in the passions of the minister. And through this process, ministers' own lives are exposed, just as the lives of others are exposed to them. If you're doing ministry with heart and soul, it's impossible to hide behind clerical trappings and religious lingo for long. The nature of the work reveals to others who you really are.

By its very nature, ministry does not fit in the box of ordination. It's a quality of caring that does not require formal training or certification. It's the expression of unconditional love which is the vocation of all Christians. A big part of my job as a professional minister is to encourage lay ministry. My job is to lift up and celebrate the many ways in which people like Ollie, without professional status, minister to others with divine compassion.

The role of the professional, ordained ministry and priesthood is changing rapidly in Christianity, precipitated by a number of historical trends. From ancient times to this century, the minister or priest was one of the very few formally educated individuals in a local community. People relied on the preacher not only to keep the church together, but to be perhaps the only source of intellectual stimulation in the town or village. The preacher was the teacher of literate culture for the local population. Studying the Bible was how many people learned to read, to study texts, to think critically and reflectively.

This situation has changed dramatically. The minister is now just one of many educated people in most local communities. Indeed, in many locales the minister has less education than a substantial percentage of the members of his or her church, and the church is just one of a great many institutions through which intellectual stimulation and cultural appreciation can be enjoyed. Secular schools can often provide a formal religious education as well as or better than churches.

Priests and ministers had other functions that are now becoming increasingly superfluous. At one time, the minister was the local public health official, inspecting the homes of parishioners for clean lifestyles. Other professionals deal with such matters today. It was not that long ago that ministers and priests were the only sources of confidential counseling, but today pastors refer their parishioners to psychotherapists and a wide variety of other specialized counselors. The only socially acceptable venue for weddings used to be the church, but today it is common for people to be married in back yards without the services of a clergy person.

Perhaps the most overlooked, yet most significant, change in the role of the ordained minister is the administrative burden of managing a parish. In the past century, the complexity of conducting the everyday business of a local church has increased tremendously. There are many more programs to be offered, more business meetings to attend, more items of paperwork to handle, more complicated building maintenance to arrange. Many churches are in denial about how much of their ministers' time is spent in administrative functions. The parish priest or minister spends most of his or her time managing a nonprofit business rather than doing ministry. Lay people must now participate in the church's pastoral activities, if for no other reason than the ordained minister is too busy managing the church office.

The most enduring role that sets the ordained minister apart from lay people is the administration of the sacraments. In most churches, it is the exclusive province of the clergy to preside over the communion or Eucharist, to baptize, and to perform marriages. But there is intense pressure to liberate these tasks from being "clergy only." As lay people obtain education comparable to or greater than clergy, there are fewer practical reasons for entrusting the sacraments solely to ordained ministers. In the Catholic Church, the number of priests is dramatically declining in industrialized nations, making it harder for the church hierarchy to resist the call from local churches to allow lay people to preach and take on other clerical functions. This is causing the Catholic Church to move slowly toward a lay-led structure in the United States.

All these changes point toward a time when ministry is no longer such a distinctly professional role, when members of a local church are empowered to care for each other at the level of the soul, to preach, teach, and conduct the rituals of the faith. Various kinds of professionals will continue to be needed to empower lay people to do ministry and to maintain the functions of church institutions. But the boundary between "clergy" and "lay people" is going to become fuzzier over time.

This change implies the emergence of a very different kind of church. It foreshadows a radical democratization of Christianity in which each individual member becomes a microcosm of the whole Christian family. It points to further fulfillment of a New Testament vision: "Like living stones, let yourselves be built into a spiritual house, to be a holy priesthood . . . in order that you may proclaim the mighty acts of him who called you out of darkness into his marvelous light." (1 Peter 2:5-9)

The present movement toward the ministry of all church members is the next step in this process of divine ordination. Lay people are now being ordained directly by God to offer spiritually centered presence and care, and to conduct the rituals of the church for each other. Whether or not we go to seminary or get certified by apostolic succession, all of us who keep the faith are likewise called by God to be ministers.

Epilogue:
A New Credo

"Jews, Christians, and Muslims know the story of the father of believers. . . . Will those who are not Jews or Christians or Muslims allow us to give Abraham's name to those minorities who are called to serve? Of course other races and religions can use an equivalent name which is more appropriate to their tradition. And you, my brothers and sisters who are atheistic humanists, don't think you have been forgotten. Translate what I say in my language into your language. When I talk of God, translate, perhaps, by 'nature,' 'evolution,' what you will. If you feel in you the desire to use the qualities you have, if you think selfishness is narrow and choking, if you hunger for truth, justice, and love, you can and should go with us."

These words of Dom Helder Camara, a Brazilian Catholic bishop, invite everyone to approach the sacred manger of Christianity as the wise men and shepherds did, even when the path seems full of insurmountable obstacles. His call to all sin-

249

cere people to join in the mission of the church was made in the context of the struggle for liberation of oppressed people in Latin America, a cause for which he risked his life and his status as a bishop.

His invitation also rings true in the context of a society in which only a minority of people maintain a meaningful affiliation with a church, and in which an increasing number of people feel alienated from the traditional doctrines of religion. Unless the church makes room for those who cannot accept orthodox dogma and ritual, there will be a constantly increasing number of people who will feel—and be—cut off from the Christian spiritual roots of Western civilization. The church needs to fling open its doors and let people enter through nontraditional translations of Christianity that make sense for them. Otherwise it will become little more than a club for history buffs, and humankind will lose access to the living spirituality it can offer.

Jesus was singularly uninterested in the doctrinal purity of the people he encountered along his road. He didn't try to edify them about correct beliefs or proper ways of performing rituals. During his lifetime, a theological debate raged between the two major factions of the educated ruling class. The Pharisees believed that the dead would be raised at judgment day, and that angels were real. The Sadducees rejected these beliefs as foolish superstitions. "Beware of the yeast of the Pharisees and the Sadducees!" warned Jesus (Matthew 16:11), metaphorically criticizing the behavior of both religious parties. His warning to avoid useless theological hairsplitting holds true today as it did then. Today, the church that was founded in his name is so busy defining who is and who is not a Christian, so distracted with its efforts to position itself in the modern marketplace of religious affiliations, that it often loses sight of the spiritual truths that created it in the first place.

The creeds of early Christianity were created primarily to settle theological and political conflicts within the church, and to establish an orthodoxy of beliefs that would help build a strong organization capable of withstanding persecution. But today, Christianity is threatened by this same orthodoxy. Many of these beliefs are now impediments to experiencing the heart of Christian faith. As one way to help get beyond these obstacles, I have written a "Credo for Christians" which summarizes the message of this book. It is an alternative to the traditional "Apostles' Creed," an expression of the enduring essence of Christian faith that dates back to the early centuries of the church. Here is the original Creed:

THE APOSTLES' CREED

I believe in God, the Father almighty,
   creator of heaven and earth.
I believe in Jesus Christ, his only Son, our Lord,
   He was conceived by the power of the Holy Spirit
      and born of the Virgin Mary.
   He suffered under Pontius Pilate,
      was crucified, died, and was buried.
   He descended to the dead.
   On the third day he rose again.
   He ascended into heaven,
      and is seated at the right hand of the Father.
   He will come again to judge the living and the dead.
I believe in the Holy Spirit,
   the holy catholic Church,
   the communion of saints,
   the forgiveness of sins,
   the resurrection of the body,
   and the life everlasting. Amen.

Here is my alternative for an Open Christianity:

A CREDO FOR CHRISTIANS

I worship and adore God, source, essence, and aim of all things,
spirit that enlivens all beings.
I follow the way of Jesus, who found God in himself
and shared a way for others to find God in themselves.
He was born through love,
He lived for love,
He suffered for love,
He died for love,
But love never dies.
I submit myself to the leading of the love that is God,
that I may be compassionate toward all beings,
that I may live and serve in community with others,
that I may ask for and offer forgiveness,
that I may praise and enjoy God forever. Amen.

Let the church open to all who seek to know God and follow the way of love, no matter what language they use to describe it. Let it open to all who seek the kind of relationship with God that Jesus had, no matter how they sort out the myths from the facts of Jesus' life story. Let those who follow a new and different Christian way find a home in the faith.

"In my Father's house there are many dwelling places. If it were not so, would I have told you that I go to prepare a place for you? And if I go and prepare a place for you, I will come again and will take you to myself, so that where I am, there you may be also." (John 14:2-3)   The one who was born in a manger, excluded from a place in the inn, promised we could join him in the presence of God. In that house there is room for everyone—traditional Christians, and those of us coming home to faith by another road, yearning to find an open door and a loving welcome at the end of our journey.

Appendices

The Eight Points of Progressive Christianity

The Center for Progressive Christianity
99 Brattle Street, Cambridge MA 02138-3402
(617) 441-0928
www.tcpc.org

By calling ourselves progressive, we mean that we are Christians who:

1. proclaim Jesus Christ as our Gate to the realm of God;

2. recognize the faithfulness of other people who have other names for the gateway to God's realm;

3. understand our sharing of bread and wine in Jesus' name to be a representation of God's feast for all peoples;

4. invite all sorts and conditions of people to join in our worship and in our common life as full partners, including (but not limited to):

    ◆ believers and agnostics

    ◆ conventional Christians and questioning skeptics,

    ◆ homosexuals and heterosexuals,

    ◆ females and males,

    ◆ the despairing and the hopeful,

    ◆ those of all races and cultures, and

    ◆ those of all classes and abilities,

    without imposing on them the necessity of becoming like us;

5. think that the way we treat one another and other people is
    more important than the way we express our beliefs;

6. find more grace in the search for meaning than in absolute
    certainty, in the questions than in the answers;

7. see ourselves as a spiritual community in which we discover
    the resources required for our work in the world:
    - striving for justice and peace among all people, and
    - bringing hope to those Jesus called the least of his sisters
      and brothers;

8. recognize that our faith entails costly discipleship,
    renunciation of privilege, and conscientious resistance to
    evil—as has always been the tradition of the church.

References and Recommended Readings

All Bible references are taken from the
New Revised Standard Version Bible, © 1989,
Division of Christian Education,
National Council of Churches of Christ in the USA.

PART I: SETTING OUT

Chapter 1. Why Another Road?

Why Christianity Must Change or Die by John Shelby Spong, Harper-SanFrancisco, 1998. This book by the Rt. Rev. Spong, Episcopal Bishop of Newark, New Jersey, is in many ways philosophically compatible with the message of *Open Christianity*. While affirming the reality of spiritual experience, he denies the historical factuality of many of the stories of Jesus' life.

Chapter 2. My Story: Discovering Open Christianity

The Journal of John Woolman, introduction by Frederick B. Tolles, Citadel Press, Carol Publishing Group, NY, 1961.

Gandhi's Autobiography: The Story of My Experiment with Truth by Mahatma Gandhi, translated by Mahadev Desai, Public Affairs Press, Washington, DC, 1960.

A Confession and Other Religious Writings by Leo Tolstoy, translated by Jane Kentish, Penguin USA, NY, 1988.

PART II: CLEARING A ROAD THROUGH CHRISTIAN TRADITIONS

Chapter 3. Keeping Faith

Transforming Christianity: Ten Pathways to a New Reformation by Stephen Glauz-Todrank, Crossroad Publishing Co., NY, 1996. A United Church of Christ pastor, the author outlines changes in direction that he sees occurring in Christianity:

- from exclusivistic to pluralistic;
- from God above to God within;
- from doctrinal to intuitional;
- from sin-based to love-based;
- from body-denying to body-affirming;
- from enfranchised to prophetic;
- from eschatological to ecological;
- from schismatic to unifying; and
- from a religion about Jesus to a religion of Jesus.

Chapter 4. God: An Introduction

Regarding Buddha and the raft: *The Enlightened Mind: An Anthology of Sacred Prose* by Stephen Mitchell, HarperCollins, NY, 1991, pp. 10-11.

Practical Mysticism: a Little Book for Normal People by Evelyn Underhill, J.M. Dent and Sons, London, E.P. Dutton & Co., NY, 1914.

Chapter 5. God: Knowing or Believing?

Regarding Yuri Gagarin declaring that he did not see God during the first manned flight into outer space: from *My Brother Yuri* by Valentin Gagarin, Progress Publishers, Moscow, 1973, p. 212.

Chapter 6. Jesus: Unique and Universal

Webster's New Collegiate Dictionary, G and C Merriam Co., Springfield, MA,1974.

Jesus: A New Vision: Spirit, Culture, and the Life of Discipleship by Marcus J. Borg, HarperSanFrancisco, 1987. One of the Jesus Seminar scholars describes the historical Jesus and the implications of his message for our time.

The Real Jesus: the Misguided Quest for the Historical Jesus by Luke Timothy Johnson, HarperSanFrancisco, 1996. A professor at the Candler School of Theology at Emory University debunks the Jesus Seminar's approach, and argues that the Jesus of faith exists in a dimension beyond the history of the first century. It is a forceful argument for a traditional Christian understanding of Jesus.

Chapter 7. Spirit: Watching Whirlwinds

The Tacit Dimension by Michael Polanyi, Doubleday Anchor, Garden City, NJ, 1967. A philosopher of science considers the role of insight and intuition in the process of discovery—a beautiful little book!

Regarding schizophrenia: *The Far Side of Madness* by John Weir Perry, Spectrum Books, Prentice-Hall, Englewood Cliffs, NJ, 1974. A Jungian psychoanalyst describes the experience of schizophrenia on its own terms, understanding it as a process that the patient needs to complete by reordering his or her cosmos.

PART III: CLEARING A ROAD THROUGH CHRISTIAN SCRIPTURES

Chapter 8. The Gospel Truth

In Parables: The Challenge of the Historical Jesus by John Dominic Crossan, Harper and Row, NY, 1973. Another member of the Jesus Seminar presents a powerful way of understanding the parables as stories that subvert conventional interpretations of the world. His tantalizing suggestion is that when Jesus was alive, he told parables; when he died, he became one.

Chapter 9. The Fig Tree: Another Reading of the Bible

Transforming Bible Study by Walter Wink, Abingdon Press, Nashville, TN, 1980. A depth-psychology approach to studying the Bible in groups.

Regarding the understanding of the eye in biblical times: *Catching the Light: The Entwined History of Light and Mind* by Arthur Zajonc, Bantam Books, NY, 1993, p. 20.

Regarding *midrashic* interpretation: *The Beginning of Desire: Reflections on Genesis* by Avivah Gottlieb Zornberg, Image Books, Doubleday, NY, 1995, p. 27.

Regarding Satan: *The Origin of Satan* by Elaine Pagels, Random House, NY, 1995. A leading scholar of the early church era outlines the development of the figure of Satan from Old Testament through medieval times.

Chapter 10. Scripture and Freedom

The Good Book: Reading the Bible with Mind and Heart by Peter J. Gomes, William Morrow and Co., NY, 1996. The minister of Memorial Church at Harvard University offers an alternative to "bibliolatry."

Regarding the history of fundamentalism in America: *Stealing Jesus: How Fundamentalism Betrays Christianity* by Bruce Bawer, Crown Publishers, NY, 1998. An unabashedly biased but very well-documented account of the background of the current effort by fundamentalist groups to establish "Christian dominion" in America.

Regarding the Baptist controversy: Cooperative Baptist Fellowship, Atlanta, GA, www.cbftexas.org/viewpoint.htm. This group broke from the Southern Baptist Convention primarily on the grounds of polity, not so much because of theological or secular political differences.

The Art of the Impossible: Politics as Morality in Practice by Vaclav Havel, Alfred A. Knopf, NY, 1997.

PART IV: OPEN CHRISTIANITY AND THE HARD QUESTIONS

Chapter 11. Death, Resurrection, and Eternal Life

Life After Life by Raymond Moody, Jr., Bantam Books, NY, 1975. This has become a classic for its descriptions of near-death experiences.

The Tibetan Book of the Dead, translated by Lama Kazi Dawa-Samdup, edited by W.Y. Evans-Wentz, with psychological commentary by C.G. Jung, Oxford University Press, NY, 1974. The after-death experiences on the *bardo* plane.

Resurrection: Myth or Reality? by John Shelby Spong, HarperSanFrancisco, 1994. A thorough historical exploration of the resurrection accounts, suggesting that while there was no physical resurrection of Jesus, the disciples had a profound Easter experience that galvanized them to create the Christian church.

Chapter 12. A New Story of the Universe

The Phenomenon of Man by Pierre Teilhard de Chardin, Perennial Library, NY, 1975. A French priest who was also a paleontologist, the author outlines a beautiful vision of the evolution of the universe toward higher levels of consciousness culminating in union with the divine.

Religion and Science: Historical and Contemporary Issues by Ian G. Barbour, HarperSanFrancisco, 1997. Barbour is perhaps the best expositor of the subject of science and religion today.

The Reenchantment of Science: Postmodern Proposals by David Ray Griffin, editor, SUNY Press, Albany, NY, 1988. This collection of essays offers hope that science and spirituality will again find common ground. Griffin is a "process theologian," interpreting the philosophy of Alfred North Whitehead, which finds common ground between quantum mechanics and spirituality.

Shadows of the Mind: A Search for the Missing Science of Consciousness by Roger Penrose, Oxford University Press, NY, 1994. One of the world's foremost mathematical physicists posits that the human mind may function not only at the electrochemical level, but at the quantum level as well.

Meister Eckhart: A Modern Translation, translated by Raymond Blakney, Harper and Row, NY, 1941 (reprinted by HarperCollins, 1986). A fourteenth-century German Catholic priest whose sermons became legendary in his time, Eckhart is an important source of inspiration for modern Christian mysticism. He was tried for heresy, but died before the Inquisition completed its case against him.

Rocks of Ages: Science and Religion in the Fullness of Life by Stephen Jay Gould, Ballantine Publishing Group, NY, 1999. An argument for separating science and religion into valid but fundamentally different pursuits.

Regarding gaps in the theory of evolution: *A Brief History of Everything* by Ken Wilber, Shambhala Publications, Boston, MA, 1996, pp. 22-23. Wilber's remarkable book is a synthesis of natural and human history, spirituality, religion, and cosmology. He is an important figure in modern transpersonal psychology.

Regarding Isaac Newton and theology: "The God of Isaac Newton" by John Brooke, in *Let Newton Be! A new perspective on his life and*

works, edited by John Fauvel, Raymond Flood, Michael Short-
land, and Robin Wilson, Oxford University Press, Oxford and
NY, 1988, p. 183.

Chapter 13. Good, Evil, and the Will of God

The Will of God by Leslie D. Weatherhead, Abingdon Press, Nashville,
TN, 1972. This classic set of sermons, written during World War
II, distinguishes between the "intentional," "circumstantial," and
"ultimate" forms of the will of God.

Letter to a Man in the Fire by Reynolds Price, Scribner, NY, 1999. A
noted writer offers a beautiful response to the questions about the
will of God asked by a man dying of cancer. Price believes that
God does personally care about and for individuals, but not all
the time—for reasons that will be eternally mysterious to us.

Chapter 14. Original Grace: The Road Beyond Sin

Adam, Eve, and the Serpent by Elaine Pagels, Vintage Books, Random
House, NY, 1988. The historical development of Christian understandings of sexuality and sin.

Chapter 15. Another Way to Face the Cross

Ego and Archetype by Edward F. Edinger for the C.G. Jung Foundation
for Analytical Psychology, G.P. Putnam's Sons, NY, 1972. This is a
Jungian view of the transformative power of Christian and other
symbols, illuminating the traditions of alchemy and homeopathy.

PART V: OPEN CHRISTIAN SPIRITUAL PRACTICE

Chapter 16. Another Road to Conversion

The Varieties of Religious Experience by William James, Longmans
Green and Co., NY, 1916. This classic in the phenomenology of
religion finds common themes in the conversion experiences of
people from many religious and personal backgrounds.

Chapter 17. Coming Home to Spiritually Centered Community

Goatwalking by Jim Corbett, Viking Press, NY, 1991. Corbett is a
Quaker cattle rancher in southern Arizona who holds a master's
degree in philosophy from Harvard. He tells the story of his
involvement in the Sanctuary Movement, interweaving it with an
analysis of the history of early Israel—a civilly disobedient and

divinely obedient people—and a unique understanding of Christianity. It is also a primer on how to live with goats in the desert wilderness.

Chapter 18. A Walk with God

A Path With Heart: A Guide Through the Perils and Promises of Spiritual Life by Jack Kornfield, Bantam Doubleday Dell Publishers, NY, 1993. A Buddhist teacher offers a primer for people on any path of spiritual discipline, with helpful practices and words of encouragement and caution.

Where People Fly and Water Runs Uphill by Jeremy Taylor, Warner Books, NY, 1992. A Unitarian minister and psychotherapist looks at the meanings in dreams, offering a practical technique for analyzing them.

Chapter 19. Coming Home to Worship

Regarding attendance at worship: "Did you really go to church this week? Behind the poll data" by C. Kirk Hadaway and Penny Long Marler, *Christian Century* magazine, Chicago, IL, May 6, 1998, pp. 472-475.

Chapter 20. Inward Mobility: Rites and Passages

"Hesitations Concerning Baptism" in *Waiting for God* by Simone Weil, G.P. Putnam's Sons, NY, 1951. Simone Weil was a French philosopher with Jewish roots. While she was never baptized into the Christian faith, her writings about Christianity place her among the foremost theologians of the twentieth century.

Chapter 21. Bread and Wine: Symbol and Reality

Regarding Lord's Supper: "Lord's Supper," article in *Columbia Encyclopedia*, Columbia University Press, NY, 1993.

Chapter 22. Another Way to Pray

Meditation: A Simple 8-Point Program for Translating Spiritual Ideals into Daily Life by Ecknath Easwaran, Nilgiri Press, Tomales, CA, 1991. An excellent primer on prayer and meditation practice for people of any religious background.

Chapter 23. Faith and Healing

The Wounded Healer: Ministry in Contemporary Society by Henri J.M. Nouwen, Image Books, Doubleday and Co., Garden City, NJ, 1972.

Chapter 24. Sacred Spaces

A Pattern Language: Towns, Buildings, Construction by Christopher Alexander, Sara Ishikawa, and Murray Silverstein with Max Jacobson, Ingrid Fiksdahl-King, and Shlomo Angel, Oxford University Press, NY, 1977, chapter 66: "Holy Ground."

Chapter 25. The Road to Nadaland

The Collected Works of St. John of the Cross, translated by Kieran Kavanaugh, OCD, and Otilio Rodriguez, OCD, Institute of Carmelite Studies, Washington, DC, 1979.

Gift of the Dark Angel by Ann Keiffer, Lura Media, San Diego, CA, 1991.

Chapter 26. Living on Humility Rock

Living Buddha, Living Christ by Thich Nhat Hanh, Riverhead Books, NY, 1997.

Chapter 27. Another Rule: From Golden to Diamond

How Can I Help? Stories and Reflections on Service by Ram Dass and Paul Gorman, Alfred A. Knopf, NY, 1985. A primer for do-gooders in how to be useful without harming those you want to help.

Chapter 28. Another Road to Soulful Sexuality

The Soul of Sex: Cultivating Life as an Act of Love by Thomas Moore, HarperCollins, NY, 1998.

Chapter 29. The Practice of Beauty

The Reenchantment of Everyday Life by Thomas Moore, HarperCollins, NY, 1998. A former monk who is now a psychotherapist outlines ways to recapture a sense of divine meaning and beauty in modern life.

PART VI: OPEN CHRISTIANITY AS LOVE IN ACTION

Chapter 30. Another Road to Christian Social Activism

We Make the Road by Walking by Myles Horton and Paulo Friere, Temple University Press, Philadelphia, PA, 1990. Two noted activists share stories and perspectives on education for social change—a primer on community organizing.

Chapter 31. Toward a New Covenant of Love

The Servant Church by Ricardo Elford and Jim Corbett, Pendle Hill Pamphlet #328, Pendle Hill Publications, Wallingford, PA, 1996. An essay on the nature of the church as a covenant community that exists beyond the bounds of institutional Christianity, written by a Catholic priest and a Quaker cattle rancher who worked together in the Sanctuary Movement in the 1980s.

Chapter 32. A Theology of *Enough*

"Jesus' New Economy of Grace" by Ched Myers in *Sojourners* magazine, Washington, DC, July-August 1998. A theology and economics of "enough," based on the biblical concepts of "Sabbath."

The Unsettling of America: Culture and Agriculture by Wendell Berry, Sierra Club Books, San Francisco, CA, 1977.

Amish Roots: A Treasury of History, Wisdom, and Lore edited by John A. Hostetler, Johns Hopkins University Press, Baltimore, MD, 1989.

Chapter 33. The Road to Vocation

The Wounded Healer: Ministry in Contemporary Society by Henri J.M. Nouwen, Image Books, Doubleday and Co., Garden City, NJ, 1972, Chapter 24.

Chapter 34. Ministry by Many: All Are Called

Ibid.

EPILOGUE: A NEW CREDO

The Desert is Fertile by Helder Camara, translated by Dinah Livingstone, Orbis Books, Maryknoll, NY, 1974.

"The Apostles' Creed" from *The Book of Common Prayer* of the Episcopal Church, 1979.

Discussion Questions
for Study Groups

Chapter 1. Why Another Road?

1. What is your relationship to the Christian religion today?

2. In what ways have you, or others you know, been helped or harmed by exposure or involvement with traditional, "closed" Christianity?

3. Do you think it is helpful or harmful to believe that Christianity is the only true religion and that Jesus Christ is the only way to salvation?

Chapter 2. My Story: Discovering Open Christianity

1. What is the story of your own faith journey? Describe the critical turning points along your way so far.

2. Where do you think your path is leading you now?

Chapter 3. Keeping Faith

1. When have you discovered that you had "raw" faith?

2. When have you discovered that you had faith "in" something or someone?

3. What makes faith "Christian"?

4. In what ways do you live "only if"?

5. In what ways do you live "as if"?

Chapter 4. God: An Introduction

1. Keep silence for at least 15 minutes, compassionately observing your own feelings and thoughts and urges. Describe this experience.

2. When and how have you directly experienced God?

3. What names do you use for God, and in which contexts do you use them?

Chapter 5. God: Knowing or Believing?

1. What God or gods don't you believe in?

2. What do you know about God, if anything?

Chapter 6. Jesus: Unique and Universal

1. What is the difference between you and your ego or personality?

2. What is the difference between Jesus and the Christ?

3. What is the difference between the Jesus you know today and the Jesus you knew as a child?

4. What aspects of the Jesus you know and love today do you consider likely to be historically accurate?

5. Does it matter to you whether or not the Jesus of your heart is the Jesus of history?

6. What is your interpretation of John 14:6: "No man comes to the Father except through me."

Chapter 7. Spirit: Watching Whirlwinds

1. When and how have you encountered Spirit?

2. When have you had to discern the difference between malevolent spirit and Holy Spirit?

3. How do your community, friends, and family help you to discern spirits?

PART III: CLEARING A ROAD THROUGH CHRISTIAN SCRIPTURES

Chapter 8. The Gospel Truth

1. How would you tell the "gospel truth" in one short paragraph?

2. Write a parable that expresses the gospel as you see it.

3. When and how have you been "gospelized"—given a window into the kingdom of heaven?

Chapter 9. The Fig Tree: Another Reading of the Bible

1. What would you have done if Dirty Bill had asked you the question about the fig tree story?

2. Has God ever spoken or written through your voice or hands? When and how have you been a channel for the Word of God?

3. Choose a passage from the New Testament and interpret it *midrashically*—freely, poetically, loosely, creatively. Try to interpret the New Testament in the same way that Jesus interpreted the Old Testament!

Chapter 10. Scripture and Freedom

1. Does the Bible have authority over your life? If so, how?

2. What is the difference between "spirituality" and "religion"?

3. What is your relationship to the Bible? How has that relationship evolved over time?

4. What kind of authority do we need in order to practice our faith?

PART IV: OPEN CHRISTIANITY AND THE HARD QUESTIONS

Chapter 11. Death, Resurrection, and Eternal Life

1. How do you view life, death, and afterlife? What personal experiences have shaped your view?

2. What do you want your own death to be like? How does this reflect what you want your life to be like?

3. In what ways have you experienced "resurrection" as part of grief?

4. Is Christian faith dependent on belief in the literal resurrection of Jesus' physical body?

5. Do you think Christianity itself needs to be resurrected from literalism?

Chapter 12. A New Story of the Universe

1. Are science and religion integrally related, or are they completely separate but equally valid ways of looking at the world?

2. What is your version of the story of the universe? How would you tell it in a few paragraphs?

3. What kind of "fish" ornaments would you put on the back of your car?

4. How does the divorce of science from religion affect your daily life? How does it affect the culture that surrounds you?

5. When have you found yourself "re-enchanted," re-connecting the physical and the spiritual dimensions of life?

Chapter 13. Good, Evil, and the Will of God

1. Tell about a time when you were sure you knew the will of God, and also about a time when your confidence in your knowledge of God's will was shattered.

2. Is evil an expression of the will of God? Or is evil our fault, a result of our fall in the Garden of Eden? Is there even such a thing as evil at all?

3. How do you discern the will of God?

Chapter 14. Original Grace: The Road Beyond Sin

1. Why did Jesus die? For your sins? Because the Romans thought he was a rabble-rouser? What does his death signify to you?

2. When have you had to take up your cross? When have you had to sacrifice your ego for the sake of love?

Chapter 15. Another Way to Face the Cross

1. Look at crucifixes or images of the cross—a variety of them, some with Jesus on them, others without. How do you feel? How does your body and soul react to each of these images?

2. What things or people in your day-to-day world are "crucifixes"?

3. How has your relationship to the image of the cross evolved over your lifetime?

PART V: OPEN CHRISTIAN SPIRITUAL PRACTICE

Chapter 16. Another Road to Conversion

1. Have you ever experienced conversion? If so, what was it like?

2. What conversion stories in other people's lives have had a profound effect on you?

Chapter 17. Coming Home to Spiritually Centered Community

1. What is your spiritual community?

2. How does your spiritual community affect your own experience of faith?

3. What are the peaks and the pitfalls of life in a church or other faith community?

Chapter 18. A Walk With God

1. What is your spiritual discipline?

2. What is difficult and what is pleasurable about it?

Chapter 19. Coming Home to Worship

1. How do your body, soul, and intellect react to worship?

2. Which parts of Christian worship are particularly meaningful and powerful for you? How does this reflect where you are on your spiritual journey?

3. Create an order of worship that you think would express your own spirituality. Then create one that you think would be meaningful to your faith community. What is the difference between the two, if any?

Chapter 20. Inward Mobility: Rites and Passages

1. What have been the most important and powerful rituals that you have gone through in your life? How did these rituals affect you?

2. Which traditional Christian rituals are most helpful and powerful for you, and which are problematic?

3. When have you seen the Spirit move among people in a ritual?

Chapter 21. Bread and Wine: Symbol and Reality

1. Share bread and wine in a group, and take special care to experience the tastes, textures, and aromas. Is Jesus present for you in this ritual? Is it real, or symbolic, for you?

2. In what ways are body and soul separated in your own life? What are the effects of this separation on your physical, emotional, and spiritual well-being?

3. What rituals or practices bring body and soul together for you?

Chapter 22. Another Way to Pray

1. Repeat the Lord's Prayer slowly, meditating on each line for a while. How does it speak for you, and in what ways does it go right over your head?

2. What is your own practice of prayer?

3. What stories can you tell about intercessory prayer (praying for others)?

4. When have you been like Hannah—waiting for an answer that never comes? And when have you been like St. Paul, letting the Spirit pray for you, letting prayer be its own answer?

Chapter 23. Faith and Healing

1. When have you experienced the difference between healing of the body and healing of the soul? And when have the two coincided?

2. Who are the healers in your life? How do they act as healers?

Chapter 24. Sacred Spaces

1. Where is your sacred space, and what is it like? What makes it sacred?

2. Design a sacred space. What are each of its elements, and what effect do these elements have in imparting the experience of the holy?

Chapter 25. The Road to Nadaland

1. What is the difference between being alone and being lonely?

2. When have you been emptied? What was it like?

3. What is your "desert"—your way to find emptiness so that you can be filled with God?

Chapter 26. Living on Humility Rock

1. When have you been humbled in your attempt to be humble? Have you ever been arrogant about your humility?

2. Have you ever sincerely believed that others will suffer damnation if they don't accept particular religious doctrines? Do you believe that now? Are any of these doctrines problematic for you?

Chapter 27. Another Rule: From Golden to Diamond

1. When have your attempts to practice the Golden Rule backfired?

2. Can you find examples in the gospels where Jesus practiced the "Diamond Rule"?

Chapter 28. Another Road to Soulful Sexuality

1. How has faith and religion affected your own sexuality, for good or ill?

2. How has faith and religion affected your view of the sexuality of others, for good or ill?

3. Based on your own positive and negative experience, what "sense education" would you like to share with your children or with others in coming generations?

Chapter 29. The Practice of Beauty

1. When have you found beauty in what the "mass culture" defines as ugly?

2.   What makes art or music "Christian"?

3.   In what ways have you become the beauty that you see?

PART VI: OPEN CHRISTIANITY AS LOVE IN ACTION

Chapter 30. Another Road to Christian Social Activism

1.   What is the connection in your own life between spirituality and work for social justice and peace?

2.   In faith communities of which you've been a part, what have been the most useful efforts for social change?

Chapter 31. Toward A New Covenant of Love

1.   Identify the areas of your life in which you live by covenant, and those you live by contract.

2.   In your community, do you see examples of people living by covenant?

3.   What role should government play in fulfilling the "100 percent covenant" of love among people?

Chapter 32. A Theology of *Enough*

1.   What factors underlie your decisions about giving to charity? How do you decide what to give, and to whom?

2.   Does your charitable giving and volunteer service outweigh the destructive impact of your consumption patterns? Or vice versa?

3.   What is the most effective charitable organization you know? What makes it so effective and efficient in use of its resources for good ends?

4.   If you assumed that everyone in the Third World was watching you all the time—how you spend money, what you eat and wear and buy, every minute—would it change how you act?

5.   Which new products and services now becoming available do you think will be beneficial to your relationships with other people, and which do you think will be harmful to those relationships?

Chapter 33. The Road to Vocation

1. Is your profession also your vocation? Is there a tension between the two? If so, what is it like?

2. What role does your vocation have in your community? How does it serve your community?

3. How does love flow through your occupation or vocation? In what new ways can love flow through it?

Chapter 34. Ministry by Many: All Are Called

1. What stories can you tell that illustrate the difference between ministry and other forms of helping relationships?

2. How are the roles of professional clergy changing? How does this affect congregations?

EPILOGUE: A NEW CREDO

1. Read the Apostles' Creed (page 251) line by line. Do you agree with each statement? Disagree? If so, what do you find troublesome?

2. Write your own "credo" for Christians. What are its connections with the doctrines of traditional Christianity, and how does it depart or evolve from them?